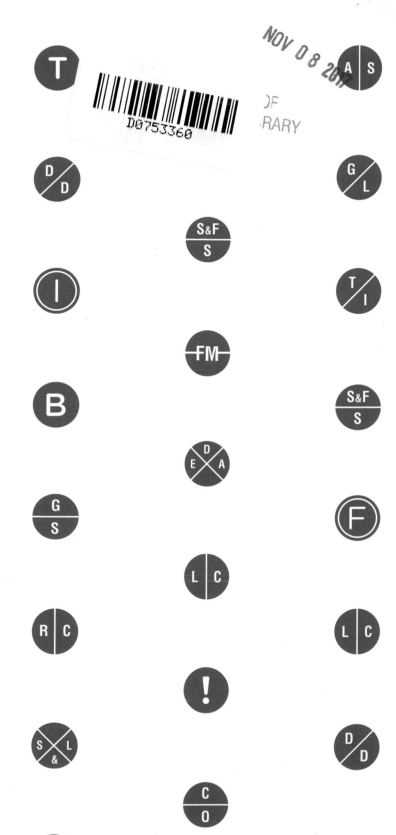

Real
PIZZA

Real
PIZZA

SECRETS OF THE
NEAPOLITAN TRADITION

MONDADORI

LEGENDA

INNOVATIVE PIZZA

INTERPRETATION
ON A CLASSIC

CLASSIC PIZZA

A DIFFERENT KIND OF PIZZA

STAFF

"MASTER" CHEF
Antonio Sorrentino
Enzo D'Angelis

PROJECT MANAGER
Roseli Katibe

COPYWRITER
Simone Natali

PHOTO
Antonio Allocca

WE WOULD LIKE TO THANK:
Clelia Martino for her valuable support
and contributions in the more than 20 years
that she has been with the Sebeto spa group.

Giorgia Mele for her collaboration and styling
support.

TRANSLATION
Mara Weiner for Language Consulting
Congressi, Milan

GRAPHIC PROJECT
jekyll & hyde

EDITING
Edizioni Il Faggio, Milan

© 2015 Mondadori Electa S.p.A, Milan
Mondadori Libri Illustrati
All rights reserved
First edition: may 2015
Second edition: december 2016

This volume was printed for Mondadori
at Elcograf S.p.A., via Mondadori 15, Verona
Printed in Italy

"
Real Neapolitan pizza is an art.
"

}  **FRANCO MANNA**

My most vivid school memories are from when I was seven years old, when pizza was the prize for a good grade or passing a class.

In those days pizzerias were few and far between, and those that did exist had been passed on from father to son. Sometimes an apprentice who had stolen his "masto's" (master's) secret would open up a new pizzeria and become the competition.

I lived in Naples, on via Cesare Rosaroll, a street without any pizzerias. There were no pizzerias on the street next to mine either, via Carbonara. The closest pizzeria was on corso Garibaldi, it was called Da Pasqualino, and that was where my mother and father would take me when I had earned a prize. It was one of those cheap places with a window onto the street that served their pizzas in the traditional Neapolitan way: "a portafoglio" (folded up like a wallet).

I will never forget the taste of that pizza. The dough was light and fragrant, the fiordilatte mozzarella mixed perfectly with the tomato, the oil and the salt. The combination of flavours was fantastic and took my breath away every time.

The secret to this magic was in the dough, and we would always talk about that secret as we sat around the marble table at Da Pasqualino. My mother would tell us about her mother's technique, which was to take the criscito (a word in dialect for natural starter yeast) and mix it with water, flour and salt. She would always stress that perfectly risen dough required lots of time.

My grandmother lived on the outskirts of the city in the town where my family was from. She wasn't a "pizzaiola" (a pizza chef) but every week she would make bread at home, or rather she would prepare the dough at home and then bake it in the communal oven in the courtyard of her building. She began making the dough on a Tuesday and, after 48 hours' rising time; it was ready for baking on a Thursday. The bread that was baked on Thursday lasted all week long and it was delicious. But the real treat for us little ones came at the end of the day, when all the leftover dough was made into pizzas and topped with fresh tomatoes, a pinch of salt and a drizzle of olive oil.

There is always a secret to pizza, whether made in a pizzeria or at home. The tastier the pizza, the more tightly held the secret, and it passes from pizzaiolo to son and mother to daughter.

Twenty years later, in 1988, I started to work in pizzerias and, with Ciro Magno, the son and grandson of pizzaioli, opened my first restaurant, Pizza e Contorni, on via Massimo Stanzione. Ten years later, in 1998, I opened the first Rossopomodoro on corso Vittorio Emanuele; today there are locations all over Naples, Milan, Rome, and even in New York, London, Riyadh, Jeddah and Reykjavík. Over the years I have heard countless stories from pizzaioli or sons and grandsons of pizzaioli, each one with their own secret for how to make the best pizza.

But what was The Secret? Was there a secret that started it all, back in the beginning – over two hundred years ago in Naples; that gave pizza its special power and made it famous the world over? I had to find out.

And I did, with a little help from my friends, chef Antonio Sorrentino and chef Enzo De Angelis. Over the last twenty years, they have helped me to improve the quality of our recipes and seek out the best suppliers and producers and in 2014 we set out on a journey to find the artisans who make the unparalleled Neapolitan pizza so great. It was a very literal journey for my friends who explored the many backstreets, districts and suburbs of Naples on the back of a Vespa. They visited historic pizzerias like Michele, Port'Alba, Sorbillo and many more. In the end they did uncover that secret, like a lost ark, and brought it back into the light of day.

Franco Manna
President of Rossopomodoro

ENZO DE ANGELIS
ANTONIO SORRENTINO
ROSSOPOMODORO CHEFS

Welcome! We are two pizza-loving Neapolitan chefs who grew up reading cookbooks and applying their wisdom in our kitchens. Our recipes were developed over many years of intense study to get just the right flavours and aromas. Pizza was always part of our world, but we really fell in love with it when we got to know the job of the pizzaiolo, the pizza maker. Even though the art of cooking and the art of making pizza are similar, true "pizzaioli" have their own philosophies, experiences and stories to share. And what stories! We were literally transported by their tales.

"Pizzaioli" tell fantastical yarns about the amazing lives they have lived. They are the keepers of knowledge that most of them began to acquire when they were very small, from parents, uncles and grandparents who were also pizzaioli.

That's because this occupation lives on solely thanks to the traditions passed down from master to apprentice; there is no need for written rules or cookbooks, just passion, talent and experience. Pizza became popular thanks the passion of "pizzaioli". It started out as a meal for the poor, but noblemen and sovereignties also appreciated this delectable dish.

From its humble origins, pizza quickly grew in popularity to become a daily part of Neapolitan life, and it wasn't long before it had taken over the world.

Come and join us as we explore first-hand the stories, recipes and places where the flavours of Neapolitan pizza are celebrated every day.

We want to "steal" their secrets so that we can make a real Neapolitan Pizza with you in your kitchen at home. Let's get started!

The beauty of pizza
lies in its simplicity.
It is born from passion and
the combination of four simple
ingredients: water, flour,
salt and yeast.

} Ⓑ THE BASICS: DOUGH

To make pizza you can use either Tipo "00" or Tipo "0", which are Italian flours milled from common wheat. These classifications of flour are based on the fineness of the milling, but if you cannot find them you can substitute them with all-purpose flour. Tipo "00", also called "doppio zero", is the easiest flour to work with. Pizzas used to be made with whole-wheat flour that was rich in fibre and protein, but that went out of fashion with the advent of refined flour, which is much easier to work with. Today many "pizzaioli" are rediscovering this old tradition and prefer to use whole-wheat flour. Whether you choose refined or whole-wheat it is important to use flour that has a high protein content, which will produce a stronger, more compact and elastic dough. Neapolitan "pizzaiolo" prefer Molino Caputo flour above all others. For three generations the same family of millers has been producing this flour. Their story began in 1924 when Carmine Caputo returned to Italy from the United States and decided to open a mill and pasta factory in the town of Capua. After Carmine passed away in 1939 his son, Antimo, bought the mill in the town of San Giovanni a Teduccio, and to this day that is where the Caputo family mills their flour. The business is now run by Antimo's sons Eugenio and Carmine, and his grandson, also called Antimo. "Simplicity" is the secret of the Caputo mill. Starting with the selection and mixing of the grains, done with great care, to get flour that is 100% natural and additive-free. Then in the milling, executed slowly so as to extract only the best parts of each grain of wheat. Many Neapolitan "pizzaioli" go in person to Molino Caputo to see up-close the production process that will give them the essential raw material, which in their hands will soon become an authentic Neapolitan pizza. And to think that in 1924 when Carmine returned to Italy his only goal was to marry his sweetheart. He achieved much more than that, but love was always the driving force.

FRESH YEAST

This yeast (also called cake yeast or brewer's yeast) is what you need to make Neapolitan pizza at home. If you have trouble finding it you can substitute it with dry active yeast. It gets the name brewer's yeast because it used to be obtained as a by-product of the beer-making process, but today it is mostly harvested from fermented sugar beets. In pizzerias, pizzaioli use a starter, which is a combination of flour and water that has been colonized by yeast spores in the air, which ferment the mixture and make the dough rise naturally.

WATER

It may seem silly to talk about water, but this is a fundamental ingredient for making a great pizza. Water is what binds the flour together with the yeast and will eventually lead to exquisite dough. The water should be moderately hard, so you have to decide if the water from your tap is good enough, or if you should use bottled water instead.

SALT

Aside from its obvious function of giving your pizza a salty taste, this ingredient also serves to inhibit the yeast and make the dough stronger. Use iodized salt and remember to always dissolve it thoroughly in water before you start to make your dough.

THE BASICS: INGREDIENTS

TOMATO

The very first Neapolitan pizzas were actually white pizzas. They were made of leftover dough from the day's bread making, to which a bit of lard or oil, salt, cheese and sometimes oregano or other herbs were added. Starting in the 1500s, imported tomatoes began to arrive from America and, well, the rest is history! Although there are thousands of varieties of tomatoes available, you should only use canned, peeled San Marzano tomatoes grown in the Campania region of Italy. For certain pizzas you can use piennolo del Vesuvio or Corbarini tomatoes, or even those little yellow ones that are more like the original tomato. One thing is certain, forget about using tomato purees!

MOZZARELLA DI BUFALA FROM CAMPANIA

Fresh buffalo mozzarella is one of the best parts of a Neapolitan pizza. Aside from its fantastic flavour, this cheese also has the advantage that it doesn't behave like other mozzarellas, and it makes pizza softer. A good tip is to always cut the cheese into slices and let any excess water drain out so that your pizza won't become soggy. You can put the cheese on your pizza however you like it best. If you like the fresh taste you can even wait until after your pizza has come out of the oven.

FIORDILATTE

Fiordilatte (cow's milk mozzarella) is another important element of Neapolitan pizza; a particularly famous variety comes from Agerola in the Campania region. The same tip we gave you before about slicing and draining also applies to this cheese.

SMOKED PROVOLONE

Smoked provolone is a special variety of cheese produced in the Campania region. Provolone is also produced from the transformation of raw cow's milk, but this variety of cheese must be stretched for longer than fiordilatte because it is supposed to be denser. Once it has reached the right consistency, the cheese is placed in a sealed environment filled with smoke produced by burning damp straw for a few minutes. This is what gives smoked provolone its distinctive flavour, colour and aroma.

BASIL

Basil (called "'a Vasinicola" in the Neapolitan dialect) is the most commonly used herb in Naples for cooking, especially the local Giant Neapolitan variety of basil. It should always be used fresh. You can put basil in your tomato sauce while you are preparing it, you can decorate your pizza with basil before you put it in the oven, and you can add fresh basil right before you serve your pizza. Basil will give your dish that special homemade touch, and its sweet, fresh smell will make your pizza even more mouth-watering.

And so it begins.
Let's set out on a journey to discover the secrets of the art of Neapolitan

pizza. Our travels will take us through the streets and alleys of Naples, from the historic city centre to the outskirts and beyond, into the countryside.

CIRO OLIVA

FROM DA CONCETTINA AI TRE SANTI

This pizza traces its roots back to Miss Concettina, the wife of a cobbler, Antonio Oliva. Like so many women in the poor neighbourhoods, she started to sell pizza to help earn money for her family.

She would sell pizza on credit, the famous ogge a otto, which meant you could eat it today and pay for it in eight days time. Thanks to her passion and the savings she amassed, the Oliva family were able to expand from their small ground floor basso into a real pizzeria that was built in 1951. It was located in the same neighbourhood where they lived, Sanità, right next to the shrine to Saints Anne, Alphonsus and Vincent. Concettina is no longer with us, but the fourth generation of pizzaioli are carrying on her tradition of making perfect, light, flavourful and affordable pizzas.

"Have fun while you're making your pizza, don't limit your creativity because no matter what the result is you'll still say, what a pizza!"

The entire Oliva family has always supported charitable work. Among the many social activities they support, they carry on the tradition of the pay-it-forward pizza, where customers pay for pizza for the hungry. They also created the Fondazione San Gennaro pizza, and every time someone orders one, they donate one Euro to the foundation to support their work caring for the homeless people who live in the neighbourhood.

PIENNOLO AND BUFALA

ingredients

- 1 BALL OF DOUGH (FOR DOUGH RECIPE SEE P. 167)
- 150 G PIENNOLO DEL VESUVIO TOMATOES
- 120 G MOZZARELLA DI BUFALA
- EXTRA VIRGIN OLIVE OIL
- GRATED PECORINO CHEESE
- NEAPOLITAN FRESH BASIL LEAVES
- SALT

PREPARING YOUR INGREDIENTS

Cut the bufala in half and then into thin slices, let any excess water drain out. Slice the little tomatoes, put them in a colander and let the water drain out. Put them into a bowl and set aside. Wash the basil and remove the leaves from the stems.

PREPARING YOUR DOUGH

Using a dough scraper lift the dough off your work surface. Quickly sprinkle it with flour and place it back on your work surface. Bring your hands together over the centre of the dough, and keeping your thumbs raised, use just your fingers to gently press the dough out moving from the centre toward the edges.
Make sure not to press down the half inch closest to the edge – this is where the air bubbles will gather to form a nice cornicione.
Stretch the pizza out by rotating your hands, always making sure not to press down on the edge.

PREPARING YOUR PIZZA

Using a spoon evenly spread the tomatoes over the stretched out dough, stopping half an inch from the edge so that the cornicione can rise during cooking. Sprinkle a little salt over the sauce and garnish with basil leaves. Lay the sliced mozzarella over the sauce in a single even layer and drizzle with extra virgin olive oil.

COOKING

Cook in a wood-fired oven or regular kitchen oven (see p. 170).

FINISHING TOUCH

Take the pizza out of the oven, drizzle with olive oil and garnish with basil.

ingredients

- 1 BALL OF DOUGH (FOR DOUGH RECIPE SEE P. 167)
- 150 G CANNED PEELED SAN MARZANO TOMATOES DOP
- 80 G PIENNOLO DEL VESUVIO TOMATOES
- 10-15 BLACK OLIVES FROM CAIAZZO
- 5-6 ANCHOVY FILLETS FROM CETARA
- A HANDFUL OF SLOW FOOD CAPERS FROM SALINA ISLAND
- 10 G EXTRA VIRGIN OLIVE OIL
- FRESH OREGANO
- NEAPOLITAN FRESH BASIL LEAVES
- SALT

} (IC) CETARESE

MARINARA WITH ANCHOVIES
AND PIENNOLO TOMATOES

PREPARING YOUR INGREDIENTS

Pour the peeled tomatoes into a bowl and mash them with your hands, then salt to taste. Slice the little tomatoes, put them in a colander and let the water drain out. Put them in a bowl and set aside. Rinse the salt off the capers. Wash the basil and remove the leaves from the stems.

PREPARING YOUR DOUGH

Using a dough scraper lift the dough off your work surface. Quickly sprinkle it with flour and place it back on your work surface. Bring your hands together over the centre of the dough, and keeping your thumbs raised, use just your fingers to gently press the dough out moving from the centre toward the edges. Make sure not to press down the half inch closest to the edge –this is where the air bubbles will gather to form a nice cornicione. Stretch the pizza out by rotating your hands, always making sure not to press down on the edge.

PREPARING YOUR PIZZA

Using a spoon evenly spread the San Marzano tomatoes over the stretched out dough, stopping half an inch from the edge so that the cornicione can rise during cooking. Sprinkle oregano over the sauce and then place the Piennolo del Vesuvio tomatoes, capers, olives and anchovies evenly across. Press down lightly on the toppings with your fingers and then season with a final dash of salt, fresh basil and a drizzle of olive oil.

COOKING

Cook in a wood-fired oven or regular kitchen oven (see p. 170).

FINISHING TOUCH

Take the pizza out of the oven and drizzle with more extra virgin olive oil, because even though this is an interpretation, a Marinara pizza always has to have lots of oil.

RESILIENZA

ingredients

- 1 BALL OF DOUGH (FOR
  DOUGH RECIPE SEE P. 167)
- PIECES OF PAPACCELLA
  PEPPER FROM
  BRUSCIANO PRESERVED
  IN OIL
- FRESH OREGANO
- CAPERS FROM SALINA
  ISLAND
- FIORDILATTE CHEESE
  WITH CAPERS
  AND OLIVES
- NEAPOLITAN BASIL
- 8-9 PITTED OLIVES
- 1 CAN OF TUNA FROM
  CETARA
- SLOW FOOD
  CACIORICOTTA CHEESE
  FROM CILENTO

PREPARING YOUR INGREDIENTS

Mash up the pepper along with any olives or capers that were preserved with it to make a paste. Cut the fiordilatte cheese into thin matchsticks and place them in a colander to let any excess water drain out.

PREPARING YOUR DOUGH

Using a dough scraper lift the dough off your work surface. Quickly sprinkle it with flour and place it back on your work surface. Bring your hands together over the centre of the dough, and keeping your thumbs raised, use just your fingers to gently press the dough out moving from the centre toward the edges. Make sure not to press down the half inch closest to the edge – this is where the air bubbles will gather to form a nice cornicione. Stretch the pizza out by rotating your hands, always making sure not to press down on the edge.

PREPARING YOUR PIZZA

Spread the pepper mixture over your stretched out dough, stopping half an inch from the edge. Crush the oregano and sprinkle it over the dough. Rinse any excess salt off the capers and evenly sprinkle them over the pizza along with the olives and a few basil leaves. Finally, top with the fiordilatte cheese and a drizzle of olive oil.

COOKING

Cook in a wood-fired or regular oven (see p. 170).

FINISHING TOUCH

Break the tuna up with a fork. Take the pizza out of the oven and sprinkle the tuna over it, then grate shavings of cacioricotta cheese from Cilento over the top.

} (DK) **CONCETTINA**

ingredients

- 1 BALL OF DOUGH (FOR DOUGH RECIPE SEE P. 167)
- 1 PORK SAUSAGE
- 300 G RAPINI
- 100 G CANNED PEELED SAN MARZANO TOMATOES
- 100 G SMOKED MOZZARELLA DI BUFALA
- 50 G RICOTTA
- 2-3 SLICES OF DRY-CURED PROSCIUTTO (CRUDO)
- SMALL CUBES OF FRIED AUBERGINE

PREPARING YOUR INGREDIENTS

Cut the smoked mozzarella di bufala into slices and let any excess water drain out. Put the San Marzano tomatoes into a bowl and mash them with your hands, then salt to taste. Wash the basil and remove the leaves from the stems. Wash the rapini and de-stem them, set aside the stems and the florets. Wash the leaves again and sauté them in a frying pan with olive oil and garlic, starting at a low flame and once they have wilted, raise the temperature for a minute and cook them uncovered. Add salt and pepper to taste. Now it's time to cook the pork sausage. Start by parboiling it and then sauté it in a frying pan with a bit of olive oil and a clove of garlic. Puncture the sausage a few times and let it cook for several minutes covered, turning the sausage over a few times so that it cooks evenly. Then add the rapini leaves into the sausage pan and let them simmer together for another couple of minutes.

PREPARING YOUR DOUGH AND YOUR PIZZA

Using a dough scraper lift the dough off your work surface and quickly sprinkle it with flour, then place it back on your work surface. Bring your hands together over the centre of the dough, and keeping your thumbs raised, use just your fingers to gently press the dough out evenly, making sure to move from the centre out toward the edges. Press out the whole circle of dough but

26

- A SLICE OF NEAPOLITAN
  CIGOLI (CRISPY PIECES
  LEFT BEHIND FROM
  RENDERING PIG FAT)
- GRATED PECORINO
  CHEESE
- PARMESAN CHEESE
  SHAVINGS
- ROCKET
- EXTRA VIRGIN OLIVE OIL
- SALT

make sure not to flatten out the half inch closest to the edge because all the air bubbles produced in the dough will concentrate here during cooking to create a nice cornicione. Shape the dough into a circle and place it onto your floured pizza peel. Using kitchen scissors make a radial cut from the right-most edge into the centre of the dough, and then evenly spread out the ricotta and cigoli over the top half of the dough and season with pepper. Now fold the right side of the dough over so that it covers the ricotta filling and gently press the edges so that it seals the cheese into the middle. You will have a C-shaped dough. Use a spoon to ladle out and spread the crushed tomatoes over the clean half of the dough, then top with the fried aubergine, a handful of rapini leaves and slices of sausage. The final touch is to put the smoked mozzarella over the top and sprinkle on some grated pecorino cheese. Drizzle over some olive oil and put it in the oven.

COOKING
Cook in a wood-fired or regular oven (see p. 170).

FINISHING TOUCH
Take the pizza out of the oven and put it on a serving dish. Decorate the empty quarter of the plate with the rocket leaves, Parmesan shavings and a rosette of dry-cured prosciutto.

! CIRO OLIVA
SAYS

When you stretch out the disc
of dough, always push with both
hands together from the centre
toward the edges. This will help
concentrate the gas bubbles,
which form while the dough rises,
into the crust. When your pizza is
cooked in the oven it will develop
a beautiful "cornicione".

Let's begin here, along the seafront.
We have our trusty Vespa, the best way to get around this city and

discover its true soul. But maybe we should have brought two!

DAVIDE CIVITIELLO
FROM ROSSOPOMODORO

Today when people talk about Rossopomodoro they aren't usually thinking of a specific restaurant in Naples. But the story does start, more than twenty years ago, with one single restaurant, on Corso Vittorio Emmanuele in Naples. It was Franco, Geppy and Pippo's fourth pizzeria and they chose a redheaded chef, the famous Ceffo, to run the restaurant. The name Rossopomodoro comes from the red of Ceffo's hair and the pizzeria's symbol, the San Marzano tomato that we use to prepare our pizzas. For Rossopomodoro, this tomato has always represented the great value of artisan products, a passion for the land and respect for tradition. Our restaurant was an immediate success and Rossopomodoro has now grown into a large family of pizzeria restaurants that serve as ambassadors of real Neapolitan pizza and cuisine throughout Italy and the world. Over the years, the story of Rossopomodoro has become intertwined with the story of Davide Civitiello, a master pizzaiolo who has honed his craft since childhood. Davide started his career at don Vincenzo Costa's pizzeria, Maddalena, and it was his experience here that united his appreciation for artisan traditions and his entrepreneurial spirit. Davide now helps to spread the passion and culture of pizza all over the world and today he has opened Rossopomodoro pizzerias in Tokyo, New York, Chicago and Jeddah. In 2013, with his long-leavened pizza, Davide became a champion for STG (Traditional Specialties Guaranteed), which recognizes the special characteristics of a product based on its place in tradition, rather than just its geographic origin.

"Put your heart into it, but no matter the result remember to smile because pizza is part of the Neapolitan spirit, which is always generous and happy?"

Back when the redheaded Ceffo was overseeing the first Rossopomodoro the locals used to say to their friends, "let's meet at Rosso's," and everyone knew what they meant. It was a name that stuck in everybody's mind!

ingredients

- 1 BALL OF DOUGH (FOR DOUGH RECIPE SEE P. 167)
- 150 G MOZZARELLA DI BUFALA FROM CAMPANIA DOP
- 130 G CANNED PEELED SAN MARZANO TOMATOES
- PENISOLA SORRENTINA EXTRA VIRGIN OLIVE OIL
- BASIL
- SALT

} VERACE

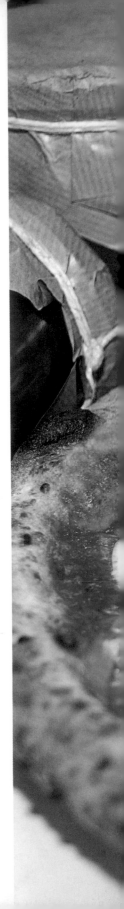

PREPARING YOUR INGREDIENTS
Put the San Marzano tomatoes into a bowl and mash them with your hands, salt to taste. Set the bowl aside. Cut the mozzarella into slices and let any excess water drain out. Wash the basil and de-stem.

PREPARING YOUR DOUGH
Using a dough scraper lift the dough off your work surface. Quickly sprinkle it with flour and place it back on your work surface. Bring your hands together over the centre of the dough, and keeping your thumbs raised, use just your fingers to gently press the dough out moving from the centre toward the edges. Make sure not to press down the half inch closest to the edge – this is where the air bubbles will gather to form a nice cornicione. Stretch the pizza out by rotating your hands , always making sure not to press down on the edge.

PREPARING YOUR PIZZA
Pour the tomato sauce onto the stretched dough, and with the back of a wooden spoon spread it over the entire pizza stopping half an inch from the edge. Sprinkle basil over the sauce and evenly lay out the slices of mozzarella.

COOKING
Cook in a wood-fired or regular oven (see p. 170).

FINISHING TOUCH
Take the pizza out of the oven, drizzle with extra virgin olive oil and garnish with fresh basil.

} (IC) **POMODOROSA**
MARGHERITA WITH
FOUR TOMATOES

ingredients
- 1 BALL OF DOUGH (FOR
  DOUGH RECIPE SEE P. 167)
- 100 G FIORDILATTE
  CHEESE
- 25 G YELLOW GRAPE
  TOMATOES
- 25 G NEAPOLITAN
  ANCIENT TOMATOES
- 25 G PIENNOLO
  DEL VESUVIO TOMATOES
- 25 G CORBARA CHERRY
  TOMATOES

PREPARING YOUR INGREDIENTS
Put each type of tomato in its own bowl and season with
a pinch of salt. Wash the basil and remove the leaves
from the stems. Cut the fiordilatte cheese into strips
and let any excess water drain out.

PREPARING YOUR DOUGH
Using a dough scraper lift the dough off your work
surface. Quickly sprinkle it with flour and place it back
on your work surface. Bring your hands together over
the centre of the dough, and keeping your thumbs
raised, use just your fingers to gently press the dough
out moving from the centre toward the edges. Make
sure not to press down the half inch closest to the edge
– this is where the air bubbles will gather to form a nice
cornicione. Stretch the pizza out by rotating your hands,
always making sure not to press down on the edge.

- GARLIC
- 10 G GRATED PECORINO
  CHEESE
- BASIL
- OREGANO
- COLLINE SALERNITANE
  EXTRA VIRGIN OLIVE OIL
- SALT

PREPARING YOUR PIZZA

Take two leftover bits of dough and roll them out to form two long cylinders and lay them across your pizza, dividing it into four equal sections. Place the Neapolitan Antique tomatoes, some fiordilatte and basil in one section. In the second section; lay out the fiordilatte and over that layer the yellow grape tomatoes. For the third section; start by layering the Piennolo del Vesuvio tomatoes and finish with three slices of garlic, a pinch of oregano and a torn basil leaf. The last section consists of Corbara cherry tomatoes and grated pecorino cheese. The final touch is a drizzle of extra virgin olive oil over the whole pizza.

COOKING

Cook in a wood-fired oven or regular kitchen oven (see p. 170).

FROM BATTIPAGLIA

ingredients

- 1 BALL OF DOUGH (FOR
  DOUGH RECIPE SEE P. 167)
- 150 G YELLOW GRAPE
  TOMATOES
- 1 CLOVE OF GARLIC
- 150 G MOZZARELLA DI
  BUFALA FROM CAMPANIA
  DOP
- EXTRA VIRGIN OLIVE OIL
  FROM THE SORRENTINE
  PENINSULA
- GROUND BLACK PEPPER
- GRATED PARMESAN
  CHEESE
- PECORINO CHEESE
- GARLIC
- BASIL
- SALT

PREPARING YOUR INGREDIENTS

Cut the mozzarella into thin slices and let any excess water drain out. Wash the basil and remove the leaves from the stems. Now make the sauce with the yellow grape tomatoes: heat some extra virgin olive oil in a small frying pan, sauté the garlic and then pour in the tomatoes. Add salt and pepper to taste and then cook for a few minutes, adding some basil for flavour.

PREPARING YOUR DOUGH

Using a dough scraper lift the dough off your work surface. Quickly sprinkle it with flour and place it back on your work surface. Bring your hands together over the centre of the dough, and keeping your thumbs raised, use just your fingers to gently press the dough out moving from the centre toward the edges. Make sure not to press down the half inch closest to the edge – this is where the air bubbles will gather to form a nice cornicione. Stretch the pizza out by rotating your hands, always making sure not to press down on the edge.

PREPARING YOUR PIZZA

Place the mozzarella slices all over the pizza, making sure to stay half an inch from the border. With a spoon spread the tomato sauce all over the cheese, sprinkle fresh basil on top and dust with grated Parmesan.

COOKING

Cook in a wood-fired oven or regular kitchen oven (see p. 170).

FINISHING TOUCH

Decorate with more fresh basil leaves and grate over a bit of pecorino cheese.

ingredients

- 1 BALL OF DOUGH (FOR DOUGH RECIPE SEE P. 167)
- 150 G OF RICOTTA (MADE FROM MOZZARELLA DI BUFALA, IF YOU CAN FIND IT)
- 100 G SMOKED MOZZARELLA DI BUFALA
- ONE LARGE SLICE OF AUBERGINE PARMIGIANA
- GRATED PARMESAN CHEESE
- EXTRA VIRGIN OLIVE OIL FROM THE SORRENTINE PENINSULA
- BASIL
- PEPPER
- SALT

 **PATCHWORK PIZZA**

PREPARING YOUR INGREDIENTS

Cut the smoked mozzarella into matchsticks and let any excess water drain out. Mix the ricotta with a wooden spatula and add salt and pepper to taste. Wash the basil and remove the leaves from the stems. Prepare a classic aubergine parmigiana.

PREPARING YOUR DOUGH

Using a dough scraper lift the dough off your work surface and quickly sprinkle it with flour, then place it back on your work surface. Bring your hands together over the centre of the dough, and keeping your thumbs raised, use just your fingers to gently press the dough out evenly, making sure to move from the centre out to the edges. Press out the whole circle of dough, even the edges.

PREPARING YOUR PIZZA

Using a spatula spread the ricotta over the dough, making sure to leave a bit extra at the edge of the pizza. Counting from the outer edge, move in one inch and sprinkle the

smoked mozzarella all over the centre of the pizza. Then sprinkle the basil, grated Parmesan cheese and ground pepper over the top. Take the edges of the dough and fold them inward creating a ricotta-stuffed crust. In the centre of the pizza add the last little bit of smoked mozzarella cheese and hand-torn pieces of aubergine parmigiana.

COOKING
Cook in a wood-fired oven or regular kitchen oven (see p. 170).

FINISHING TOUCH
When you take your pizza out of the oven decorate it with more basil leaves.

! DAVIDE CIVITIELLO
SAYS

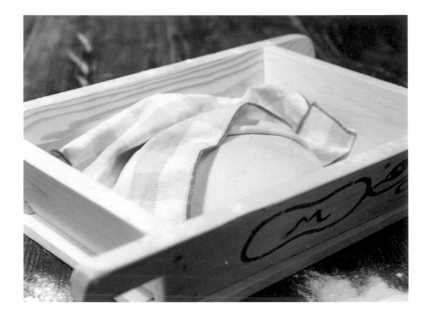

Take your time! Dough rises
for a long time in a pizzeria,
sometimes up to 24 hours.
At home you can reduce the
amount of yeast you use and try
to let your dough rise for
at least 8 hours.
This will make your pizza lighter
and easier to digest.

let's meet

DOMENICO DE LUCA

FROM PELLONE

This historic pizzeria opened in 1960 on the street that leads to Piazza Nazionale. It was the labour of love of Vincenzo, brother to Concetta, the mother of the De Luca brothers. It started out as a hole-in-the-wall neighbourhood pizzeria, and the owner's only ambition was to make good, honest pizza. It was the De Luca brothers who changed all that, turning this humble establishment into one of the most well known pizzerias in Naples, and the world. Franco and Antimo were just kids when they started working in their uncle's restaurant, doing everything from hosting and cooking to administering the place. Meanwhile their elder brother Mimmo was following his dream of being a cook in Tuscany. After their uncle became ill, and seeing that the "pizzaioli" who used work alongside him were unable to keep the place going, the De Luca brothers decided to take the reins. Despite their youth, the brothers had a clear idea about what they wanted for their future: to stay together and make simple, genuine, high-quality food. Thanks to their great tenacity, their pizza grew ever more popular, earning them the nickname "e' guagliune" (handsome guys, in Neapolitan dialect), and finally in the 1990s Pellone pizzeria really took off. Today, the enormous pizzas that overhang their plates, the appetisers, the fried pizzas, and all the other delicious dishes draw clients into this restaurant at every hour of the day – and night!

"Pizza is like a lady, you must love her, respect her, treat her well, and fill her with passion."

"Pizzaioli" care deeply about the traditions of their art, and you can see that here in the old framed poem from the 1800s in which the author says, "of this beautiful Naples and my past in it, no memory remains," but Franco Mimmo and Antimo have added, "(what do you mean no memory!)... only a pizza and nothing else remains."

} Ⓒ CAPRICCIOSA

ingredients

- 1 BALL OF DOUGH (FOR
  DOUGH RECIPE SEE P. 167)
- 100 G CANNED PEELED
  SAN MARZANO TOMATOES
- 80 G AGEROLA
  FIORDILATTE CHEESE
- 2 SLICES OF HAM STEAK
  (PROSCIUTTO COTTO)
- 50 G BUTTON
  MUSHROOMS SAUTÉED
  WITH BUTTER
  AND PARSLEY
- 7-8 BLACK OLIVES

PREPARING YOUR INGREDIENTS

Slice the fiordilatte and let any excess water drain out. Place the San Marzano tomatoes into a bowl and mash them with your hands, add salt to taste. Wash the basil and remove the leaves from the stems.

PREPARING YOUR DOUGH

Using a dough scraper lift the dough off your work surface. Quickly sprinkle it with flour and place it back on your work surface. Bring your hands together over the centre of the dough, and keeping your thumbs raised, use just your fingers to gently press the dough out moving from the centre toward the edges. Make sure not to press down the half inch closest to the edge – this is where the air bubbles will gather to form a nice cornicione. Stretch the pizza out by rotating your hands, always making sure not to press down on the edge.

- 1-2 ARTICHOKES
  PRESERVED IN OIL
  AND SLICED
- BASIL
- GRATED PECORINO AND
  PARMESAN CHEESES
- EXTRA VIRGIN OLIVE OIL
- SALT

PREPARING YOUR PIZZA

Using a spoon spread the San Marzano tomatoes evenly over your dough, making sure to stay half an inch away from the edge. Evenly layer the mushrooms, fiordilatte, artichokes, prosciutto cotto and pitted black olives over the sauce. Sprinkle the grated cheese mix over the toppings and decorate with fresh basil and a drizzle of extra virgin olive oil.

COOKING

Cook in a wood-fired oven or regular kitchen oven (see p. 170).

MARINARA
WITH FRESH ANCHOVIES

} (IC)

ingredients

- 1 BALL OF DOUGH (FOR
  DOUGH RECIPE SEE P. 167)
- CANNED PEELED
  SAN MARZANO
  TOMATOES
- FRESH ANCHOVIES
- EXTRA VIRGIN OLIVE OIL
- BASIL
- GARLIC
- OREGANO
- SALT

PREPARING YOUR INGREDIENTS

Put the San Marzano tomatoes into a bowl and mash them with your hands, then salt to taste. Peel the garlic and cut it into rounds . Wash the basil and remove the leaves from the stems. Wash the anchovies, remove the heads and guts, and rinse them once more. Store them in the fridge.

PREPARING YOUR DOUGH

Using a dough scraper lift the dough off your work surface. Quickly sprinkle it with flour and place it back on your work surface. Bring your hands together over the centre of the dough, and keeping your thumbs raised, use just your fingers to gently press the dough out moving from the centre toward the edges. Make sure not to press down the half inch closest to the edge – this is where the air bubbles will gather to form a nice cornicione. Stretch the pizza out by rotating your hands, always making sure not to press down on the edge.

PREPARING YOUR PIZZA

Using a spoon spread the tomatoes over the dough, and layer on the garlic rounds , fresh anchovies, oregano and lots of torn basil. Drizzle with a generous amount of extra virgin olive oil.

COOKING

Cook in a wood-fired oven or regular kitchen oven (see p. 170).

① 'A MASTU CICCIO

ingredients

- 1 BALL OF DOUGH (FOR DOUGH RECIPE SEE P. 167)
- 500 G PEELED PUMPKIN
- 2 SMALL SAUSAGES
- 100 G EXTRA VIRGIN OLIVE OIL
- 100 G SMOKED MOZZARELLA DI BUFALA
- A SLICE OF ONION
- 1 GARLIC CLOVE
- GRATED PECORINO AND PARMESAN CHEESES
- BASIL
- SALT

PREPARING YOUR INGREDIENTS

Sauté your pumpkin as follows: cut the pumpkin it into small cubes. In a frying pan heat 50 g of olive oil and sauté the sliced onion until it starts to turn translucent, then add the cubed pumpkin. Cook for several minutes, stirring a few times, and then pour in enough water to cover the single layer of pumpkin. Add a pinch of salt and reduce the liquid, lightly braising the pumpkin. Now it's time to cook the small pork sausages. Start by parboiling them and then sauté them in a frying pan with a bit of olive oil and a clove of garlic. Puncture the sausages a few times and let them cook for several minutes covered, turning them over a few times so that they cook evenly. Cut the smoked mozzarella di bufala into wide matchsticks and let any excess water drain out. Wash the basil and remove the leaves from the stems.

PREPARING YOUR DOUGH

Using a dough scraper lift the dough off your work surface. Quickly sprinkle it with flour and place it back on your work surface. Bring your hands together over the centre of the dough, and keeping your thumbs raised, use just your fingers to gently press the dough out moving from the centre toward the edges. Make sure not to press down the half inch closest to the edge – this is where the air bubbles will gather to form a nice cornicione. Stretch the pizza out by rotating your hands, always making sure not to press down on the edge.

PREPARING YOUR PIZZA

Using a spoon spread the pumpkin evenly over your dough, making sure to stay half an inch away from the edge. Crumble your sausages into large chunks and spread them over the pumpkin, then layer over the smoked mozzarella di bufala. Sprinkle the grated cheese mix over the top and decorate with fresh basil.

COOKING

Cook in a wood-fired or regular oven (see p. 170).

FINISHING TOUCH

Take your pizza out of the oven and garnish with basil.

ingredients

- 1 BALL OF DOUGH (FOR
  DOUGH RECIPE SEE P. 167)
- 150 G MOZZARELLA
  DI BUFALA FROM
  CAMPANIA DOP
- 1 RED TROPEA ONION
- 1 OXHEART TOMATO
  FROM SORRENTO
- ROCKET
- EXTRA VIRGIN OLIVE OIL
- BASIL
- OREGANO
- SALT

} (DK) **PAN PELLONE**

PREPARING YOUR INGREDIENTS

Wash the tomato and cut it into slices. Wash the rocket.
Peel the Tropea onion and cut it into slices. Cut the
mozzarella in half and then into slices, so as to get
a half-moon shape.

PREPARING YOUR DOUGH

Using a dough scraper lift the dough off your work
surface and quickly sprinkle it with flour, then place it
back on your work surface. Bring your hands together
over the centre of the dough, and keeping your thumbs
raised, use just your fingers to gently shape the dough
into a large flat circle, pressing evenly all the way to
the edge. Put the dough on a floured pizza peel. Before
putting it in the oven drizzle a bit of olive oil over the
dough and fold it in half, achieving a half-moon shape.
Then press down gently on the folded edge, but not on
the circular border.

COOKING
Cook in a wood-fired oven or regular kitchen oven
(see p. 170).

FINISHING TOUCH
Take your "pan Pellone" (Pellone bread) out of the oven
and slice it open like pita bread. Stuff it with tomato
slices lightly dressed with olive oil, salt, basil
and oregano. Then on top of the tomatoes layer the slices
of mozzarella di bufala and onion. Sprinkle over some
rocket leaves and a generous amount of olive oil.
Close the pizza back up and garnish with basil.

! DOMENICO DE LUCA
SAYS

Pizza dough should be thin
when it is stretched out, as we
say in Naples, "fine 'e pasta,"
thin as dough.

If you ask a local for directions in Naples they'll start to give you instructions

and before you know it, they're accompanying you to where you need to go.

FERDINANDO DE GIULIO
FROM ERMENEGILDO

"It used to be that you would order your pizza based on how much change you had in your pocket, 'make me one that's worth...' – how much? It's up to you to decide, and have fun making it at home!"

As you walk up to the entrance of this enormous pizzeria in San Giovanni a Teduccio, on the outskirts of Naples, you will smell the aroma of the frying dough that made this family famous. Ermenegildo De Giulio started out selling pizza from a cart that he took all over the city, and when itinerant food sellers were banned, he opened his restaurant. Ermenegildo's five sons followed him into the trade and have maintained the old traditions. They are bound together by their love of this Neapolitan speciality of fried pizza. They still prepare everything by hand using the specialised tools that their father invented and made, like the long rods and perforated pallets they use to nimbly move the dough around in the hot oil, which they like to specify is not boiling. Their fried pizzas are delicious to eat and beautiful to behold; they fry up thousands of them each week, sometimes even for breakfast!

Ermenegildo was so determined to keep making pizza that he built this entire place by hand. He even broke a few laws doing it, which led to delays, during which time he and his family had to live in a potato storeroom. But, he didn't give up and he made his dream come true: he built a wonderful "pizzeria".

ingredients

- 2 BALLS OF DOUGH,
  125 G EACH (FOR RECIPE
  SEE P. 167)
- 2 LARGE SPOONFUL'S
  OF TOMATO SAUCE
  PREPARED WITH CANNED
  PEELED TOMATOES,
  GARLIC, OLIVE OIL, BASIL
- GRATED PARMESAN
  CHEESE
- BASIL
- SEED OIL FOR FRYING

FOR THE FILLING:
- 100 G GOAT'S MILK
  RICOTTA FROM
  SORRENTO
- 50 G SMOKED
  MOZZARELLA DI BUFALA
- 2 SLICES OF PORK CIGOLI
- PEPPER
- SALT

VESUVIUS
OF NAPLES

PREPARING YOUR INGREDIENTS

Pour the oil for frying into a large pot with high sides
and heat until it reaches 180 °C (356 °F). Wash the basil
and remove the leaves from the stems. Cut the smoked
mozzarella di bufala into matchsticks and let any excess
water drain out. Pour the ricotta into a bowl, add a
pinch of salt and mix it well with a wooden spatula.

PREPARING AND STUFFING YOUR DOUGH

Using a dough scraper lift the dough off your work
surface and quickly sprinkle it with flour. Cover your
work surface with a clean tea towel and place the dough
on the towel. This will help keep the dough from
sticking to your work surface. Bring your hands together
over the centre of the dough, and keeping your thumbs
raised, use just your fingers to gently press the dough
out evenly all the way to the edges. Press out your dough
until you have made it the size that you want, then set
aside on a floured surface and repeat these steps with
your second ball of dough. Choose one of your disks of
dough and spread your ricotta, mozzarella, cigoli (broken
up with your hands) and two spoonful's of tomato sauce

all over it, seasoning with pepper. Then cover it with the
second disk of dough and press all the edges down with
your fists so that they stick together creating a seal.

COOKING

Gently lower your pizza into the hot oil and with the
help of a long spatula hold it in place. Use a skimmer to
pour hot oil over the surface of the pizza so that it turns
golden on both sides. The pizza will start to expand.
Remove the pizza from the oil and place it on a plate
lined with kitchen roll to gather any excess oil.

FINISHING TOUCH

Pour a spoonful of tomato sauce over the centre of the
pizza, grate Parmesan cheese over the top, and decorate
with basil.

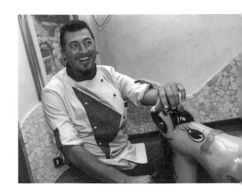

MONTANARA WITH TOMATO SAUCE AND GOAT'S MILK RICOTTA

IC

ingredients

- 1 BALL OF DOUGH, 150 G
  (FOR RECIPE SEE P. 167)
- 30 G GOAT'S MILK
  RICOTTA FROM
  SORRENTO
- 1 SPOONFUL OF ALREADY
  PREPARED TOMATO
  SAUCE (MADE WITH
  CANNED PEELED
  TOMATOES, GARLIC
  AND OLIVE OIL)
- GRATED PARMESAN
  CHEESE
- BASIL
- SEED OIL FOR FRYING
- SALT

PREPARING YOUR INGREDIENTS

Pour the oil for frying into a large pot with high sides and heat the oil until it reaches 180 °C (356 °F). Wash the basil and remove the leaves from the stems. Pour the ricotta into a bowl, add a pinch of salt and mix it well with a wooden spatula.

PREPARING YOUR DOUGH

Using a dough scraper lift the dough off your work surface and quickly sprinkle it with flour. Cover your work surface with a clean tea towel and place the dough on the towel. This will help keep the dough from sticking to your work surface. Bring your hands together over the centre of the dough, and keeping your thumbs raised, use just your fingers to gently press the dough out evenly all the way to the edges. Set aside on a plate in preparation for frying.

COOKING

Gently lower your pizza into the hot oil and with the help of a long spatula hold it in place. Use a skimmer to pour hot oil over the surface of the pizza so that it turns golden on both sides. The pizza will start to expand. Remove the pizza from the oil and place it on a plate lined with kitchen roll to gather any excess oil.

FINISHING TOUCH

Pour the ricotta over the surface of the fried pizza and spread out evenly, then do the same with a spoonful of tomato sauce, grate fresh Parmesan cheese over the top and decorate with basil.

} ◯ **PORCONA**

ingredients

- 1 BALL OF DOUGH, 300 G
  (FOR RECIPE SEE P. 167)
- 1 SPOONFUL OF ALREADY
  PREPARED TOMATO
  SAUCE (MADE WITH
  CANNED PEELED
  TOMATOES, GARLIC,
  OLIVE OIL AND FRESH
  BASIL)
- GRATED PARMESAN
  CHEESE
- BASIL
- SEED OIL FOR FRYING
- SALT

PREPARING YOUR INGREDIENTS

Pour the oil for frying into a large pot with high sides and heat until it reaches 180 °C (356 °F). Cut the smoked mozzarella di bufala into matchsticks and let any excess water drain out. Wash the basil and remove the leaves from the stems.

PREPARING AND STUFFING YOUR DOUGH

Using a dough scraper lift the dough off your work surface and quickly sprinkle it with flour. Cover your work surface with a clean tea towel and place the dough on the towel. This will help keep the dough from sticking to your work surface. Bring your hands together over the centre of the dough, and keeping your thumbs raised, use just your fingers to gently press the dough out evenly all the way to the edges. Press out your dough until you have made it the size that you want. Spread the smoked mozzarella over half of the disk of dough, making sure to stop half an inch in from the edge. Over the top of the cheese; layer on the sliced porchetta, pieces of hand-torn prosciutto and the mushrooms. Grate over fresh Parmesan and a few basil leaves. Grab the dough at the edges where the saucy side meets the empty side and pull it a bit so that the dough becomes oval-shaped. Fold

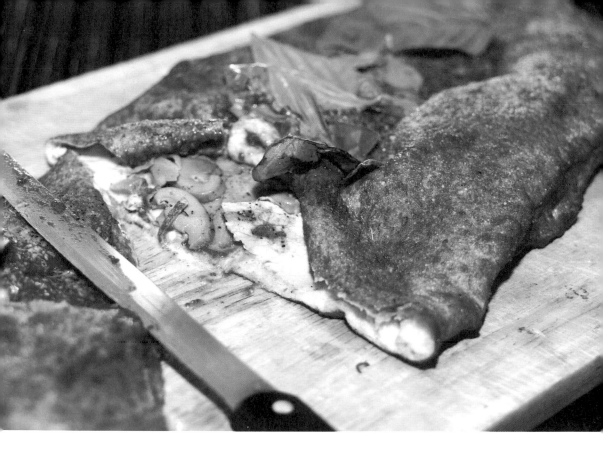

FOR THE FILLING:
- 50 G SLICED PORCHETTA
- 50 G SMOKED MOZZARELLA
- 30 G BUTTON MUSHROOMS SAUTÉED
- A SLICE OF HAM STEAK (PROSCIUTTO COTTO)
- BLACK PEPPER
- OIL FOR FRYING

the empty side over the topped half and, using your fists to press it down at the edges; create a seal.

COOKING
Gently lower your pizza into the hot oil and with the help of a long spatula hold it in place. Use a skimmer to pour hot oil over the surface of the pizza. The pizza will start to expand. Once it has turned golden on one side turn the pizza over in the oil so it turns golden on the other side. Remove the pizza from the oil and place it on a plate lined with kitchen roll to gather any excess oil.

FINISHING TOUCH
Put the pizza on a serving dish and ladle a spoonful of sauce over the long side. Dust with ground pepper, freshly grated Parmesan and garnish with basil.

} (DK) THE SUN

ingredients

- 2 BALLS OF DOUGH,
  150 G EACH (FOR RECIPE
  SEE P. 167)
- PARMESAN CHEESE
  SHAVINGS
- SEED OIL FOR FRYING

FOR THE FILLING:
- 2 BUNCHES OF RAPINI
- 2 FRESH PORK SAUSAGES
- 50 G SMOKED
  MOZZARELLA
- RICOTTA
- PEPPER
- GRATED PARMESAN
  CHEESE
- GARLIC
- EXTRA VIRGIN OLIVE OIL
- BASIL
- PEPPER
- HOT PEPPER (OPTIONAL)
- SALT

PREPARING YOUR INGREDIENTS

Wash the rapini and de-stem them, set aside the stems and the florets. Wash the leaves again and sauté them in a frying pan with olive oil and garlic, starting at a low flame and then once they have wilted raise the temperature for a minute and cook them uncovered. Add salt and pepper to taste. Now it's time to cook the pork sausage. Start by parboiling it and then sauté it in a frying pan with a bit of olive oil and a clove of garlic. Puncture the sausage a few times and let it cook for several minutes covered, turning the sausage over a few times so that it cooks evenly. Then add the rapini leaves into the sausage pan and let them simmer together for another couple of minutes. Wash the basil and remove the leaves from the stems. Cut the smoked mozzarella di bufala into matchsticks and let any excess water drain out. Pour the ricotta into a bowl, add a pinch of salt and mix it well with a wooden spatula. Pour the oil for frying into a large pot with high sides and heat until it reaches 180°C (356°F).

PREPARING AND STUFFING YOUR DOUGH

Using a dough scraper lift the dough off your work surface and quickly sprinkle it with flour. Cover your work surface with a clean tea towel and place the dough on the towel. This will help keep the dough from sticking to your work surface. Bring your hands together over the centre of the dough, and keeping your thumbs raised, use just your fingers to gently press the dough out evenly all the way to the edges. Press out your dough until you have made it the size that you want, then set aside on a floured surface and repeat these steps with your second ball of dough. Choose one of your disks of dough and evenly spread out the rapini, then spoonful's of ricotta, the smoked mozzarella, round slices of sausage, the Parmesan cheese and a dash of ground pepper. Cover with the other disc of dough and use your fists to seal the edges. Using a pair of kitchen scissors make short (half inch, or less) cuts into the dough. Do this around the entire edge of the pizza at regular intervals, making sure not to cut through to the filling so that you leave the toppings completely sealed in the centre.

COOKING

Gently lower your pizza into the hot oil and with the help of a long spatula hold it in place. Use a skimmer to pour hot oil over the surface of the pizza. The pizza will start to expand. Once it has become golden on one side, turn the pizza over in the oil so it becomes golden on the other side. Remove the pizza from the oil and place it on a plate lined with kitchen roll to gather any excess oil.

FINISHING TOUCH

Decorate your sun with a sprig of rapini, a spoonful of ricotta and Parmesan cheese shavings.

FERDINANDO DE GIULIO
SAYS

When preparing fried pizza, stretch your dough out on a clean, cotton tea towel so that it absorbs any moisture. This way the dough won't stick to your work surface and there won't be any water to come into contact with the hot oil.

We can "speak" in Japanese, Russian, German and English because foreign tourists always understand Neapolitans.

She said it was good so let's go in!

let's meet

GINO SORBILLO

FROM SORBILLO

Located in the heart of old Naples, Sorbillo's friendly atmosphere is evident even before you walk through the flower-filled entrance. Part of the charm of this pizzeria comes from the family that runs it, led by the father Luigi Sorbillo and his 21 children, all "pizzaioli". One among the brood is Gino Sorbillo, a "pizzaiolo" who is famous all over the world thanks to his appearances on Masterchef Italia and Australia. Then there is Antonio Sorbillo, Gino's right hand man, who early each morning prepares the day's dough. He also runs the register, manages the dining room, and in his free time he boxes. Every day the owner, Anna Sorbillo, Gino and Antonio welcome their customers in this warm, historic restaurant where the art of making pizza is inherited, but passion elevates it to a profession.

"When preparing your pizza try to be original. Put your heart into it and you get even better!"

Today, in the house that used to belong to their aunt Esterina, they have opened the "House of Pizza," where the spirit of the people combines with the soul of the city to form a place dedicated to family, pizza and, of course, Naples.

} © **ROUND CALZONE**

ingredients
- 2 BALLS OF DOUGH (FOR
  RECIPE SEE P. 167)

FOR THE FILLING:
- 50-60 G CANNED PEELED
  SAN MARZANO
  TOMATOES
- 120 G MOZZARELLA
  DI BUFALA FROM
  CAMPANIA DOP
- BASIL
- SALT

PREPARING YOUR INGREDIENTS
Put the San Marzano tomatoes into a bowl and
mash them with your hands, then salt to taste. Cut
the mozzarella in half and then into either slices or
matchsticks, whatever you prefer, and let any excess
water drain out. Wash the basil and remove the leaves
from the stems.

PREPARING YOUR DOUGH
Using a dough scraper lift the dough off your work
surface and quickly sprinkle it with flour, then place it
back on your work surface. Bring your hands together
over the centre of the dough, and keeping your thumbs
raised, use just your fingers to gently shape the dough
into a large flat circle, pressing evenly all the way to the
edge. Repeat with your second ball of dough.

PREPARING YOUR PIZZA
Choose one of your discs of dough and sprinkle the
mozzarella evenly over its surface, keeping away from
the edges, then spoon the tomato sauce over the cheese.
Place your second disc of dough over the top, matching
up the edges. Using your fists press the edges of the

FOR THE OUTSIDE:
- A SPOONFUL OF CANNED
  PEELED SAN MARZANO
  TOMATOES DOP
- PARMIGIANO REGGIANO
  DI MONTAGNA CHEESE
- BLACK PEPPER
- BUFALA RICOTTA
  (OPTIONAL)
- EXTRA VIRGIN OLIVE OIL
- BASIL
- SALT

two discs of dough together, creating a good seal. Now gently move your stuffed dough onto a floured pizza peel and decorate the top with a thin layer of tomato sauce. Sprinkle grated Parmesan cheese and pepper over the top and drizzle with olive oil.

COOKING
Cook in a wood-fired oven or regular kitchen oven
(see p. 170).

FINISHING TOUCH
Take your pizza out of the oven and garnish with fresh basil. You can also garnish it with salted and peppered bufala ricotta.

MARGHERITA FROM CORBARA

{ (IC)

ingredients

- 1 BALL OF DOUGH (FOR DOUGH RECIPE SEE P. 167)
- 130 G FRESH FIORDILATTE CHEESE
- 100 G FRESH BUFALA RICOTTA
- 10 CORBARA CHERRY TOMATOES PRESERVED IN SALT WATER
- EXTRA VIRGIN OLIVE OIL
- BASIL
- SALT

PREPARING YOUR INGREDIENTS

Drain the Corbara cherry tomatoes, place them into a bowl and gently mash them. Cut the fiordilatte into matchsticks and let any excess water drain out. Pour the ricotta into a bowl, add a pinch of salt and mix it well with a wooden spatula. Wash the basil and remove the leaves from the stems.

PREPARING YOUR DOUGH

Using a dough scraper lift the dough off your work surface. Quickly sprinkle it with flour and place it back on your work surface. Bring your hands together over the centre of the dough, and keeping your thumbs raised, use just your fingers to gently press the dough out moving from the centre toward the edges. Make sure not to press down the half inch closest to the edge – this is where the air bubbles will gather to form a nice cornicione. Stretch the pizza out by rotating your hands, always making sure not to press down on the edge.

PREPARING YOUR PIZZA

Spread the ricotta over the dough with a spatula making sure to stay half an inch away from the edge. Place the Corbara cherry tomatoes over the ricotta and decorate with fresh basil. Cover the pizza with the fiordilatte cheese and drizzle with a generous amount of olive oil.

COOKING

Cook in a wood-fired oven or regular kitchen oven (see p. 170).

TORZELLA

ingredients

- 1 BALL OF DOUGH (FOR DOUGH RECIPE SEE P. 167)
- 140 G OF TORZELLE (ANCIENT BROCCOLI) PRESERVED IN WATER AND OIL
- FRESH FIORDILATTE CHEESE
- 5 SLICES OF PEPPERED BACON
- EXTRA VIRGIN OLIVE OIL
- BASIL
- SALT

PREPARING YOUR INGREDIENTS

Cut the fiordilatte cheese into matchsticks and let any excess water drain out. Drain the liquid from the torzelle. Wash the basil and remove the leaves from the stems.

PREPARING YOUR DOUGH

Using a dough scraper lift the dough off your work surface. Quickly sprinkle it with flour and place it back on your work surface. Bring your hands together over the centre of the dough, and keeping your thumbs raised, use just your fingers to gently press the dough out moving from the centre toward the edges. Make sure not to press down the half inch closest to the edge – this is where the air bubbles will gather to form a nice cornicione. Stretch the pizza out by rotating your hands, always making sure not to press down on the edge.

PREPARING YOUR PIZZA

Lay out the torzelle leaves in a single layer over the dough, making sure to stay away from the edges. Evenly sprinkle the fiordilatte cheese on top and drizzle with extra virgin olive oil.

COOKING

Cook in a wood-fired or regular oven (see p. 170).

FINISHING TOUCH

Take the pizza out of the oven and put the slices of bacon on top. The heat will melt the fat on the bacon, making your pizza even tastier.

(DK) 'NDUJA HEART

ingredients

- 1 BALL OF DOUGH (FOR DOUGH RECIPE SEE P. 167)
- 120 G MOZZARELLA DI BUFALA FROM CAMPANIA DOP
- 100 G 'NDUJA (A SPICY, SPREADABLE PORK SAUSAGE)
- 70 G PORCINI MUSHROOMS SAUTÉED
  - PECORINO BAGNOLESE CHEESE
- EXTRA VIRGIN OLIVE OIL
- BASIL
- SALT

PREPARING YOUR INGREDIENTS

Cut the mozzarella di bufala into slices and let any excess water drain out. Mash the 'nduja sausage until it turns into a creamy paste. Wash the basil and remove the leaves from the stems.

PREPARING YOUR DOUGH

Using a dough scraper lift the dough off your work surface and quickly sprinkle it with flour, then place it back on your work surface. Bring your hands together over the centre of the dough, and keeping your thumbs raised, use just your fingers to gently press the dough out evenly, making sure to move from the centre out toward the edges. Press out the whole circle of dough but make sure not to flatten out the half inch closest to the edge where all the air bubbles will concentrate to form the cornicione. Shape the dough into a large circle and then holding one edge still, take the opposite side of the dough and gently pull it away from the centre of the pizza, creating a pointy end. Now take the rounded lip on the opposite side of the circle and push it toward the centre with one finger, this way you will create a heart-shaped dough. Place the dough onto your floured pizza peel.

PREPARING YOUR PIZZA

Using a spatula spread the 'nduja paste over the dough, making sure to stay half an inch from the edge. Evenly lay the sautéed mushrooms over the sausage and sprinkle with basil. Cover the pizza in mozzarella di bufala and drizzle with extra virgin olive oil.

COOKING

Cook in a wood-fired oven or regular kitchen oven (see p. 170).

FINISHING TOUCH

Take your pizza out of the oven and decorate with shavings of pecorino Bagnolese cheese.

! GINO SORBILLO
SAYS

Dissolve the yeast in a bit of water before putting it into your dough mixture, that way it will be absorbed evenly.

let's meet

GENNARO LUCIANO

FROM ANTICA PIZZERIA PORT'ALBA

Port'Alba is one of the ancient gates of Naples; it is the main access route to the Decumano Maggiore. Right at its base you will find one of the oldest pizzerias in the city, named after the famous gateway. Run by Gennaro Luciano, he is the fourth generation of his family to run this business that is said to have started as far back as 1738 as a prep kitchen for the itinerant "ogge a otto" (eat now, pay in eight days) pizza salesmen. In 1830 it became a real pizzeria, and today is recognized as the oldest pizzeria in Naples, and the world! Inside you will find an endless array of antique pizza making tools, which are still used today –in as much as the new health laws allow – as part of the pizzaioli's efforts to remain faithful to tradition. Even the oven is the same. Gennaro has hundreds of tales to tell, starting with the story of his family and his father Vincenzo, who began to teach Gennaro this trade at the tender age of 13, and whose life's work has been recognised with the title of Cavaliere del Lavoro (Order of Merit for Labour), for his contributions to the art of making pizza. Today hundreds of customers, especially students from the nearby university flock to fill the tables of this establishment, or take their pizza to go, folded up "a portafoglio", as tradition dictates.

"Make pizza with your children and grandchildren; it will be a great life lesson, because it teaches you how to put love into what you do."

So many famous characters have visited this ancient pizzeria, like Salvatore di Giacomo, Benedetto Croce and Gabriele D'Annunzio, who, as legend has it, wrote the lyrics to the famous Neapolitan song "'A Vucchella" (with music by Francesco Paolo Tosti) while sitting at one of these tables!

} © ROMAN PIZZA

IN OTHER PARTS OF
ITALY IT IS CALLED
NEAPOLITAN PIZZA

ingredients

- 1 BALL OF DOUGH (FOR
  DOUGH RECIPE SEE P. 167)
- 120 G CANNED PEELED
  SAN MARZANO
  TOMATOES
- 100 G AGEROLA
  FIORDILATTE CHEESE
- 5 FILLETS OF ANCHOVIES
  FROM CETARA
  PRESERVED IN OIL

PREPARING YOUR INGREDIENTS

Cut the fiordilatte into slices and let any excess water
drain out. Put the San Marzano tomatoes into a bowl
and mash them with your hands, then salt to taste. Wash
the basil and remove the leaves from the stems.

PREPARING YOUR DOUGH

Using a dough scraper lift the dough off your work
surface. Quickly sprinkle it with flour and place it back
on your work surface. Bring your hands together over
the centre of the dough, and keeping your thumbs
raised, use just your fingers to gently press the dough
out moving from the centre toward the edges. Make
sure not to press down the half inch closest to the edge
– this is where the air bubbles will gather to form a nice
cornicione. Stretch the pizza out by rotating your hands,

- GRATED PECORINO
  BAGNOLESE CHEESE
- EXTRA VIRGIN OLIVE OIL
  FROM BENEVENTO
- BASIL
- SALT

always making sure not to press down on the edge.

PREPARING YOUR PIZZA
Spread the San Marzano tomatoes evenly over your dough, making sure to stay half an inch away from the edge. Drain the anchovies of most of their oil and lay them over the sauce. Sprinkle some fresh basil, the fiordilatte slices and the grated pecorino cheese over the top and drizzle with olive oil.

COOKING
Cook in a wood-fired oven or regular kitchen oven (see p. 170).

PORT'ALBA

MARINARA WITH SEAFOOD

ingredients

- 1 BALL OF DOUGH (FOR
  DOUGH RECIPE SEE P. 167)
- 150 G CANNED PEELED
  SAN MARZANO
  TOMATOES
- 1 GARLIC CLOVE
- OREGANO
- BASIL
- EXTRA VIRGIN OLIVE OIL

FOR THE SEAFOOD SAUTÉ:
- 100 G MUSSELS
- 3 SMOOTH CLAMS
- 100 G CLAMS
  (ALL CLEANED)
- CLEANED SQUID
- 2 SHRIMP
- 4-5 PIENNOLO DEL
  VESUVIO TOMATOES
- ONE CLOVE OF GARLIC
- HOT RED PEPPER
- PARSLEY
- EXTRA VIRGIN OLIVE OIL
- SALT

PREPARING YOUR INGREDIENTS

Put the San Marzano tomatoes into a bowl and mash them with your hands, then salt to taste. Peel the garlic and slice it thin. Wash the basil and remove the leaves from the stems. Prepare the sautéed seafood: finely chop the parsley and rinse the seafood one more time. Cut the squid into rounds . Rinse the Piennolo del Vesuvio tomatoes and cut them in half. Take the clove of garlic that still has its peel and pound it well a few times. Heat some olive oil in a frying pan and, leaving the skin on, sauté the garlic adding the ground hot red pepper to taste. Push the garlic to one side of the pan and pour in the squid, shrimp and all the other shellfish. Cook until the shells open and then add in the halved tomatoes and reduce the liquid. Sprinkle with finely chopped parsley and turn the burner off.

PREPARING YOUR DOUGH

Using a dough scraper lift the dough off your work surface. Quickly sprinkle it with flour and place it back on your work surface. Bring your hands together over the centre of the dough, and keeping your thumbs raised, use just your fingers to gently press the dough out moving from the centre toward the edges. Make sure not to press down the half inch closest to the edge – this is where the air bubbles will gather to form a nice cornicione. Stretch the pizza out by rotating your hands, always making sure not to press down on the edge.

PREPARING YOUR PIZZA

Using a spoon spread the San Marzano tomatoes evenly over the dough, then top with finely sliced garlic, fresh oregano, basil and a drizzle of olive oil.

COOKING

Cook in a wood-fired oven or regular kitchen oven (see p. 170).

FINISHING TOUCH

Take your pizza out of the oven and put it on a serving dish. Ladle the seafood sauté over the pizza, staying away from the edges, and sprinkle with parsley.

DON GENNARO

ingredients

- 1 BALL OF DOUGH (FOR DOUGH RECIPE SEE P. 167)
- AGEROLA PROVOLONE CHEESE
- 1 AUBERGINE
- 1 COURGETTE
- BLACK GAETA OLIVES
- GRANA CHEESE AGED 24 MONTHS
- EXTRA VIRGIN OLIVE OIL FROM BENEVENTO
- BASIL
- OREGANO
- PEPPER
- SALT

PREPARING YOUR INGREDIENTS

Cut the provolone cheese into wide matchsticks and let any excess water drain out. Wash the basil and remove the leaves from the stems. Remove the pits from the olives, cut the aubergine and courgette into thin slices and grill. Dress the grilled vegetables with some olive oil, salt, oregano and basil.

PREPARING YOUR DOUGH

Using a dough scraper lift the dough off your work surface. Quickly sprinkle it with flour and place it back on your work surface. Bring your hands together over the centre of the dough, and keeping your thumbs raised, use just your fingers to gently press the dough out moving from the centre toward the edges. Make sure not to press down the half inch closest to the edge – this is where the air bubbles will gather to form a nice cornicione. Stretch the pizza out by rotating your hands, always making sure not to press down on the edge.

PREPARING YOUR PIZZA
Lay slices of provolone cheese in a single layer all over
the pizza, making sure to stay half an inch from the
edge. Sprinkle over the Grana shavings and grind pepper
over the top. Then add a few basil leaves and
a drizzle of olive oil.

COOKING
Cook in a wood-fired oven or regular kitchen oven
(see p. 170).

FINISHING TOUCH
Take your pizza out of the oven and place on a serving
dish. Top the pizza with the slices of grilled vegetables,
pitted olives, more fresh basil and crushed hot red
pepper to taste.

ingredients

- 1 BALL OF DOUGH (FOR DOUGH RECIPE SEE P. 167)
- 100 G AGEROLA RICOTTA (COW'S MILK)
- 80 G AGEROLA PROVOLONE CHEESE
- 60 G YELLOW CHERRY TOMATO PRESERVES
- 3 SLICES OF SMOKED BACON
- GRANA CHEESE THAT HAS BEEN AGED FOR 24 MONTHS
- SHAVINGS OF PECORINO CHEESE
- BLACK PEPPER
- EXTRA VIRGIN OLIVE OIL
- BASIL
- SALT

THE SUN IN THE MOON

PREPARING YOUR INGREDIENTS

Cut the provolone cheese into wide matchsticks and let any excess water drain out. Pour the ricotta into a bowl and add a pinch of salt and pepper, then mix it well with a wooden spatula. Put the tomatoes into a bowl and press them lightly, then dress them with salt and a bit of extra virgin olive oil. Wash the basil and remove the leaves from the stems.

PREPARING YOUR DOUGH

Using a dough scraper lift the dough off your work surface and quickly sprinkle it with flour, then place it back on your work surface. Bring your hands together over the centre of the dough, and keeping your thumbs raised, use just your fingers to gently shape the dough into a large flat circle, pressing evenly all the way to the edge.

PREPARING AND STUFFING YOUR PIZZA

On one half of your dough evenly spread a base of ricotta, then sprinkle half of your provolone cheese, the slices of

bacon, grated Grana and the ground black pepper. Take the plain half of your dough and fold it over the other side. Seal the edges well with your fingers, creating a half-moon shape. Using a spoon spread the yellow cherry tomato sauce over the top of the dough and layer over the rest of the provolone cheese, the pecorino shavings, basil and a drizzle of olive oil.

COOKING
Cook in a wood-fired oven or regular kitchen oven (see p. 170).

FINISHING TOUCH
Take your pizza out of the oven and garnish with basil.

! GENNARO LUCIANO
SAYS

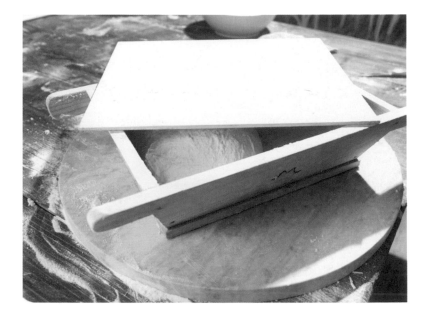

Get a wooden bowl because
dough left to rest in wood will
be less moist and will yield
a more fragrant pizza.

Residents of the "bassi" (typical ground floor apartments in poor, crowded neighbourhoods) spend most of the day at their windows. They

are often elderly, tell stories, keep secrets and love gossip, so when they give you advice you should always take it. Let's keep going that way!

LUIGI CONDURRO
FROM ANTICA PIZZERIA MICHELE

When you walk into this old pizzeria you get the feeling that you're entering a space untouched by the passage of time. There are beautiful vintage furnishings, marble tabletops and giant poetic verses dedicated to pizza across the wall. Since 1870 six generations of Condurro family "pizzaioli" have pulled pizzas out of the ovens in this restaurant that has been called by many experts "the sacred temple of pizza." Michele was the great master pizzaiolo who taught so many Neapolitan "pizzaioli" their craft. After him came Salvatore, Antonio and Luigi who helped the business grow into what it is today. The pizza is still made according to the traditions set down by Michele, who only wanted to make two kinds of pizza: Marinara and Margherita. The Cosacca pizza is made only upon request, and legend has it that this variety was invented by Michele's grandfather who offered it as a gift to Czar Nicholas II on his visit to Naples.

"Pizza needs light! It must be seen and admired attentively like a masterpiece, both while it is being made and while it is being eaten."

In the movie "Fat, Pray, Love", the American director Ryan Murphy and the great actress Julia Roberts tell a story that highlights how it is possible to find happiness by surrendering to the pleasures of food, like the delicious Neapolitan pizza the protagonist eats at Michele's pizzeria.

MARGHERITA

ingredients

- 1 BALL OF DOUGH (FOR DOUGH RECIPE SEE P. 167)
- 120 G CANNED PEELED SAN MARZANO TOMATOES
- 100 G AGEROLA FIORDILATTE CHEESE
- GRATED PECORINO CHEESE
- EXTRA VIRGIN OLIVE OIL
- BASIL
- SALT

PREPARING YOUR INGREDIENTS

Cut the fiordilatte into matchsticks and let any excess water drain out. Put the San Marzano tomatoes into a bowl and mash them with your hands, then salt to taste. Wash the basil and remove the leaves from the stems.

PREPARING YOUR DOUGH

Using a dough scraper lift the dough off your work surface. Quickly sprinkle it with flour and place it back on your work surface. Bring your hands together over the centre of the dough, and keeping your thumbs raised, use just your fingers to gently press the dough out moving from the centre toward the edges. Make sure not to press down the half inch closest to the edge – this is where the air bubbles will gather to form a nice cornicione. Stretch the pizza out by rotating your hands, always making sure not to press down on the edge.

PREPARING YOUR PIZZA

Using a spoon spread the San Marzano tomatoes evenly over your dough, making sure to stay half an inch away from the edge, and then layer fresh basil and the fiordilatte cheese on top of the sauce. Drizzle over some olive oil and sprinkle the grated pecorino on top.

COOKING

Cook in a wood-fired oven or regular kitchen oven (see p. 170).

FINISHING TOUCH

Take your pizza out of the oven and garnish with basil.

ingredients

- 1 BALL OF DOUGH (FOR DOUGH RECIPE SEE P. 167)
- 150 G CANNED PEELED SAN MARZANO TOMATOES
- GARLIC
- OREGANO
- EXTRA VIRGIN OLIVE OIL
- BASIL
- SALT

} **MARINARA**

PREPARING YOUR INGREDIENTS

Put the San Marzano tomatoes into a bowl and mash them with your hands, then salt to taste. Peel the garlic and cut it into slices. Wash the basil and remove the leaves from the stems.

PREPARING YOUR DOUGH

Using a dough scraper lift the dough off your work surface. Quickly sprinkle it with flour and place it back on your work surface. Bring your hands together over the centre of the dough, and keeping your thumbs raised, use just your fingers to gently press the dough out moving from the centre toward the edges. Make sure not to press down the half inch closest to the edge – this is where the air bubbles will gather to form a nice cornicione. Stretch the pizza out by rotating your hands, always making sure not to press down on the edge.

PREPARING YOUR PIZZA

Using a spoon spread the San Marzano tomatoes evenly over your dough, making sure to stay half an inch away from the edge, and then layer over the garlic, basil, oregano and a generous amount of oil.

COOKING

Cook in a wood-fired oven or regular kitchen oven (see p. 170).

} IC COSACCA

ingredients

- 1 BALL OF DOUGH (FOR
  DOUGH RECIPE SEE P. 167)
- 130 G CANNED PEELED
  SAN MARZANO
  TOMATOES
- GRATED PECORINO
  CHEESE
- EXTRA VIRGIN OLIVE OIL
- BASIL
- SALT

PREPARING YOUR INGREDIENTS
Put the San Marzano tomatoes into a bowl and mash
them with your hands, then salt to taste. Wash the basil
and remove the leaves from the stems.

PREPARING YOUR DOUGH
Using a dough scraper lift the dough off your work
surface. Quickly sprinkle it with flour and place it back
on your work surface. Bring your hands together over
the centre of the dough, and keeping your thumbs
raised, use just your fingers to gently press the dough
out moving from the centre toward the edges. Make
sure not to press down the half inch closest to the edge
– this is where the air bubbles will gather to form a nice
cornicione. Stretch the pizza out by rotating your hands,
always making sure not to press down on the edge.

PREPARING YOUR PIZZA
Using a spoon spread the San Marzano tomatoes evenly
over your dough, making sure to stay half an inch away
from the edge.
Sprinkle over a generous amount of grated pecorino
cheese, a drizzle of olive oil and basil.

COOKING
Cook in a wood-fired oven or regular kitchen oven
(see p. 170).

FINISHING TOUCH
Take your pizza out of the oven and sprinkle over more
grated pecorino cheese.

ingredients

- 1 BALL AND HALF OF
  DOUGH (FOR RECIPE
  SEE P. 167)
- 130 G CANNED PEELED
  SAN MARZANO
  TOMATOES
- 50-60 G AGEROLA
  FIORDILATTE CHEESE
- GRATED PECORINO
  CHEESE
- GARLIC
- OREGANO
- EXTRA VIRGIN OLIVE OIL
- BASIL
- SALT

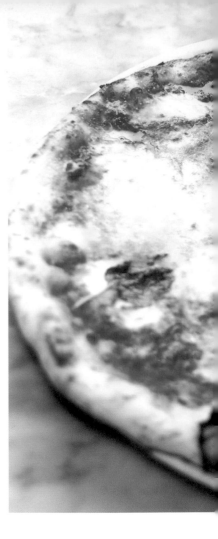

} (DK) **HALF AND HALF**

HALF MARGHERITA
AND HALF MARINARA

PREPARING YOUR INGREDIENTS

Put the San Marzano tomatoes into a bowl and mash
them with your hands, then salt to taste. Cut the
fiordilatte into slices and let any excess water drain out.
Peel the garlic and cut it into matchsticks. Wash the basil
and remove the leaves from the stems.

PREPARING YOUR DOUGH

Using a dough scraper lift the dough off your work
surface. Quickly sprinkle it with flour and place it back
on your work surface. Bring your hands together over
the centre of the dough, and keeping your thumbs
raised, use just your fingers to gently press the dough
out moving from the centre toward the edges. Make
sure not to press down the half inch closest to the edge
– this is where the air bubbles will gather to form a nice
cornicione. Stretch the pizza out by rotating your hands,
always making sure not to press down on the edge.

Take a bit of dough from another unused ball of dough and rolling it between the work surface and the palms of your hands make a long, thin piece of dough to divide your pizza in half. Using a spoon spread the San Marzano tomatoes evenly over one half of your dough, making sure to stay half an inch away from the edge, fiordilatte slices , then sprinkle this side with grated pecorino cheese. Spread the remaining tomatoes over the other half of the pizza and sprinkle it with the sliced garlic, basil, oregano and olive oil.

COOKING
Cook in a wood-fired oven or regular kitchen oven (see p. 170).

! LUIGI CONDURRO
SAYS

Listen to what your hands
are telling you.
They are essential tools
for feeling when you have
achieved the right consistency,
or "punto di pasta",
when your dough is soft,
dry and compact.

Naples is a city of contrasts:

everything and its opposite can be found here. So let's split up!

RAIMONDO CINQUE
FROM GIGINO PIZZA A METRO

It was here, at Vico Equense, on the Sorrentine coast in the 1930s that the baker Gigino Dell'Amura, motivated by poverty and the need to feed his workers and seven children, invented a practical and easy dish. He wanted to add variety to their traditional diet of bread and vegetables. Using some of his dough, he started to make a single, huge pizza. He topped it with lots of different ingredients, and cut it into slices so everyone could eat. This wasn't your normal pizza; using the knowledge he had gained as a baker he chose his ingredients carefully, from the flour to the yeast. But his long pizza still didn't have a special name. It was the artist and conductor of the Vienna Chamber Orchestra, maestro Carlo Zecchi, a frequent patron of Gigino's, who after seeing the length of the pizzas asked for one a metre long so he could feed the whole orchestra! And that's how the name Pizza a Metro (pizza by the metre) was born. Ever since then the Dell'Amura family has baked kilometres and kilometres of pizza, and today Gigino's sons Antonio, Francesco, Carlo, Giulio and Mario carry on the family business. There are so many things that make these pizzas unique, as the owner Luigi Dell'Amura and the "pizzaiolo" Raimondo Cinque explain, starting from the thick, soft dough to the generous toppings, to the longer rising and cooking times, all of these elements combine to create a pizza that will suit any taste!

> **"Make simple pizza. Always use authentic ingredients, but remember to keep your spirit humble!"**

During the war Gigino, like all bakers, had the job of giving bread to the poor when they presented him with their ration cards, but each person was only supposed to receive a small amount. Often his compassion and desire to give poor customers a reason to smile led him to give quite a bit more bread than they were supposed to receive. He did so at great personal risk, he could have been arrested or jailed!

 MARGHERITA

ingredients

INGREDIENTS FOR THE
DOUGH:
- 1 KG WHOLE WHEAT
  FLOUR TIPO "0" (IF YOU
  CANNOT FIND THIS YOU
  CAN USE ALL-PURPOSE
  WHOLE-WHEAT FLOUR)
- 720 ML WATER
- 30 G SALT
- 4 G FRESH YEAST

INGREDIENTS FOR
THE TOPPINGS:
- 500 G AGEROLA
  FIORDILATTE CHEESE
  CUT INTO CUBES
- 350 G CANNED PEELED
  SAN MARZANO
  TOMATOES
- 150 G GRATED PARMESAN
  CHEESE
- 70 G LARD MELTED
  IN A DOUBLE BOILER
- BASIL
- SALT

MAKING THE DOUGH

In a large mixing bowl dissolve the salt and yeast in room temperature water, then add the flour and mix well. Knead the dough for 20 minutes and then let it rise for five hours.

PREPARING YOUR DOUGH AND YOUR INGREDIENTS

After the dough has risen for five hours separate out a ball of dough that weighs approximately 750 g and let it rest for 15 minutes. Sprinkle flour on your work surface and on your ball of dough, then roll it out using a rolling pin. Put the dough on an oiled baking sheet and spread the fiordilatte cheese over it, then the San Marzano tomatoes, sprinkle the grated Parmesan and finally pour over the melted lard and decorate with basil.

COOKING

Cook in a wood-fired oven or regular kitchen oven (see p. 170).

ingredients

INGREDIENTS FOR THE
DOUGH:
- 1 KG FLOUR TIPO "00"
  (IF YOU CANNOT FIND
  THIS YOU CAN USE ALL-
  PURPOSE FLOUR)
- 720 ML WATER
- 30 G SALT
- 4 G FRESH YEAST

INGREDIENTS FOR
THE TOPPING:
- 800 G ESCAROLE
  WASHED, CLEANED
  AND FINELY CHOPPED
- 650 G CHERRY TOMATOES
  CUT IN HALF
- 300 G GAETA OLIVES
- 100 G CAPERS
- 70 G EXTRA VIRGIN
  OLIVE OIL
- BASIL

MARGHERITA WITH ESCAROLE

MAKING THE DOUGH
In a large mixing bowl dissolve the salt and yeast in room temperature water, then add the flour and mix well. Knead the dough for 20 minutes and then let it rise for five hours.

PREPARING YOUR DOUGH AND YOUR INGREDIENTS
After the dough has risen for five hours separate out a ball of dough that weighs approximately 750 g and let it rest for 15 minutes. Sprinkle flour on your work surface and on your ball of dough, then roll it out using a rolling pin. Put the dough on an oiled baking sheet and evenly layer the escarole, pitted olives, capers, tomatoes and basil on top, and drizzle with olive oil.

COOKING
Cook in a wood-fired oven or regular kitchen oven (see p. 170).

SCALLION AND GUANCIALE

ingredients

INGREDIENTS FOR
THE DOUGH:
- 1 KG WHOLE WHEAT
  FLOUR TIPO "0" (IF YOU
  CANNOT FIND THIS YOU
  CAN USE ALL-PURPOSE
  WHOLE-WHEAT FLOUR)
- 720 ML WATER
- 30 G SALT
- 4 G FRESH YEAST

INGREDIENTS FOR
THE TOPPING:
- 700 G THINLY SLICED
  GUANCIALE (CURED
  PORK CHEEK)
- 500 G AGEROLA
  FIORDILATTE CHEESE
- 300 G SHAVINGS
  OF GRANA PADANO
  CHEESE
- 1 SCALLION
- BASIL

MAKING THE DOUGH

In a large mixing bowl dissolve the salt and yeast in
room temperature water, then add the flour and mix
well. Knead the dough for 20 minutes and then let
it rise for five hours.

PREPARING YOUR DOUGH AND YOUR INGREDIENTS

After the dough has risen for five hours separate out a
ball of dough that weighs approximately 750g and let it
rest for 15 minutes. Sprinkle flour on your work surface
and on your ball of dough, then roll it out using a rolling
pin. Put the dough on an oiled baking sheet and spread
slices of guanciale over it, then layer the fiordilatte,
Grana Padana shavings, sliced scallion and some
basil on top.

COOKING

Cook in a wood-fired oven or regular kitchen oven
(see p. 170).

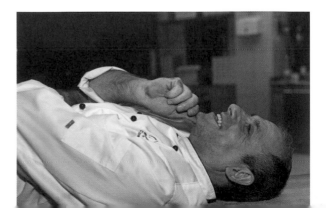

} (DK) CORNUCOPIA

ingredients

INGREDIENTS FOR
THE DOUGH:
- 1 KG FLOUR TIPO "00"
  (IF YOU CANNOT FIND
  THIS YOU CAN USE ALL-
  PURPOSE FLOUR)
- 720 ML WATER
- 30 G SALT
- 4 G FRESH YEAST

INGREDIENTS FOR
THE TOPPING:
- 400 G ESCAROLE
  WASHED, CLEANED
  AND FINELY CHOPPED
- 350 G MOZZARELLA
  DI BUFALA FROM
  CAMPANIA DOP
- 350 G TOMATOES FROM
  SORRENTO
- 250 G RICOTTA
- 170 G EXTRA VIRGIN
  OLIVE OIL
- 100 G GAETA OLIVES
- 50 G CAPERS
- 50 G SHAVINGS OF
  PARMESAN CHEESE
- ROCKET
- SALT
- PEPPER
- BASIL

MAKING THE DOUGH

In a large mixing bowl dissolve the salt and yeast in room temperature water, then add the flour and mix well. Knead the dough for 20 minutes and then let it rise for five hours.

PREPARING YOUR DOUGH AND YOUR INGREDIENTS

After the dough has risen for five hours separate out a ball of dough that weighs approximately 750 g and let it rest for 15 minutes. In the meantime sauté the escarole in a frying pan with olive oil, then add the olives and capers. Cut the tomatoes into cubes. Sprinkle flour on your work surface and on your ball of dough, then roll it out using a rolling pin. Put the dough on a baking sheet and cover the first quarter section with ricotta and pepper, then the next quarter section with half of tomatoes and half of the mozzarella, and the third quarter section with the sautéed escarole, olives and capers. Now take the edge of the pizza and roll it over to the other side covering the ingredients you just laid out. This will create a horn like a cornucopia with one end closed and the other open. Lightly oil the dough and sprinkle Parmesan on top.

COOKING

Cook in a wood-fired oven or regular kitchen oven (see p. 170).

FINISHING TOUCH

Top the open part of the pizza with rocket, cherry tomatoes dressed with olive oil and oregano, and decorate with Parmesan cheese shavings.

! RAIMONDO CINQUE
SAYS

You must use room-temperature water to make good dough.

Everyone knows the local traditions, even the kids. Neapolitans can rattle off popular sayings, sing old songs and they love traditional recipes.

Everyone knows that Neapolitan pizza is supposed to be eaten with your hands, holding it closed "a portafoglio" (folded up), according to tradition.

SALVATORE & FRANCESCO SALVO

FROM SALVO

When you enter "Salvo", in the town of San Giorgio a Cremano, you will immediately notice their motto, "Innovation is Tradition." Salvatore and Francesco, the brothers who run this place, have combined their family's traditions with a great curiosity for new developments in cooking. They hail from a long line of pizzaioli that began with their grandmother who sold fried pizza right from her basso, or ground floor apartment. Then there was their grandfather and his thirteen brothers, all pizzaioli. But it was their father, Giuseppe Salvo, who opened the family's first pizzeria, in the town of Portici. In 2006 Salvo moved to its current location where they welcome diners from all over the province!

> "Make pizza if it was the first thing on your mind when you woke up, and enjoy it in good company!"

To this day their father, Giuseppe, is still affectionately remembered for his fantastically risen dough, which he used to sell from a cart on the street when he was just starting out. Many of his old patrons and friends still come to enjoy this pizzeria's delicious treats and fondly remember their great maestro and friend.

MARGHERITA FROM VESUVIUS

ingredients

- 1 BALL OF DOUGH
  (FOR RECIPE SEE P. 167)
- 150 G CANNED PIENNOLO
  DEL VESUVIO TOMATOES
- 150 G MOZZARELLA DI
  BUFALA FROM
  CAMPANIA DOP
- 10 G EXTRA VIRGIN OLIVE
  OIL FROM VESUVIUS
- BASIL
- SALT

PREPARING YOUR INGREDIENTS

Pour the tomatoes into a colander and let the liquid drain away, then lightly salt them to taste and set them aside in a bowl. Cut the mozzarella into slices and let any excess water drain out. Wash the basil and remove the leaves from the stems.

PREPARING YOUR DOUGH

Using a dough scraper lift the dough off your work surface. Quickly sprinkle it with flour and place it back on your work surface. Bring your hands together over the centre of the dough, and keeping your thumbs raised, use just your fingers to gently press the dough out moving from the centre toward the edges. Make sure not to press down the half inch closest to the edge – this is where the air bubbles will gather to form a nice "cornicione". Stretch the pizza out by rotating your hands, always making sure not to press down on the edge.

PREPARING YOUR PIZZA

Gently mash your tomatoes in the bowl and then ladle them onto your dough. Use the back of your spoon to spread them evenly over the dough, stopping half an inch from the edge, so that the cornicione can rise during cooking. Place slices of mozzarella evenly over the sauce and drizzle olive oil over them, then sprinkle with basil.

COOKING

Cook in a wood-fired oven or regular kitchen oven (see p. 170).

FINISHING TOUCH

Drizzle your pizza with extra virgin olive oil before serving.

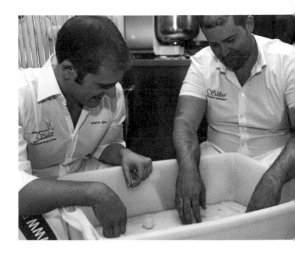

COSACCA WITH CORBARINO AND PECORINO

IC

ingredients

- 1 BALL OF DOUGH (FOR
  RECIPE SEE P. 167)
- 150 G CORBARA CHERRY
  TOMATOES
- 70 G RAW MILK PECORINO
  BAGNOLESE CHEESE
- COLLINE SALERNITANE
  EXTRA VIRGIN OLIVE OIL
- BASIL
- SALT

PREPARING YOUR INGREDIENTS

Put the tomatoes into a bowl and mash them, then
season them to taste.

PREPARING YOUR DOUGH

Using a dough scraper lift the dough off your work
surface. Quickly sprinkle it with flour and place it back
on your work surface. Bring your hands together over
the centre of the dough, and keeping your thumbs
raised, use just your fingers to gently press the dough
out moving from the centre toward the edges. Make
sure not to press down the half inch closest to the edge
– this is where the air bubbles will gather to form a nice
cornicione. Stretch the pizza out by rotating your hands,
always making sure not to press down on the edge.

PREPARING YOUR PIZZA

After stretching out your dough, ladle a generous
amount of the tomatoes on top and spread out with the
back of a spoon. Top with basil and extra virgin olive oil.

COOKING

Cook in a wood-fired oven or regular kitchen oven
(see p. 170).

FINISHING TOUCH

Remove your pizza from the oven and grate a generous
amount of pecorino over the top, then finish with
a drizzle of extra virgin olive oil.

PAPACCELLE PEPPER AND CONCIATO ROMANO CHEESE

ingredients

- 1 BALL OF DOUGH (FOR DOUGH RECIPE SEE P. 167)
- 90-100 G FIORDILATTE CHEESE FROM CAMPANIA
- 120 G OF PAPACCELLE (NEAPOLITAN PEPPERS) GRILLED AND PRESERVED IN OIL
- 25-30 G OF CONCIATO ROMANO CHEESE
- 10 G EXTRA VIRGIN OLIVE OIL
- SALT

PREPARING YOUR INGREDIENTS
Cut the fiordilatte like matchsticks and let any excess water drain out. Drain most of the oil from the peppers and set them aside in a bowl.

PREPARING YOUR DOUGH
Using a dough scraper lift the dough off your work surface. Quickly sprinkle it with flour and place it back on your work surface. Bring your hands together over the centre of the dough, and keeping your thumbs raised, use just your fingers to gently press the dough out moving from the centre toward the edges. Make sure not to press down the half inch closest to the edge – this is where the air bubbles will gather to form a nice cornicione. Stretch the pizza out by rotating your hands, always making sure not to press down on the edge.

PREPARING YOUR PIZZA
Lay the peppers out over the dough in a single layer
making sure to stay half an inch from the edge.
Then sprinkle over the cut up fiordilatte and drizzle with
olive oil.

COOKING
Cook in a wood-fired oven or regular kitchen oven
(see p. 170).

FINISHING TOUCH
Remove your pizza from the oven and use a mandolin
grater to cover your pizza in shavings of conciato
Romano cheese. Decorate with a final touch of extra
virgin olive oil.

ingredients

- A 280 G BALL OF DOUGH
  (FOR RECIPE SEE P. 167)
- 150 G "FAKE" GENOVESE
  SAUCE (USE 4 KG OF
  COPPER-SKINNED ONIONS
  FROM MONTORO, CELERY,
  CARROTS, 200 G EXTRA
  VIRGIN OLIVE OIL, BASIL,
  WHITE WINE, SALT)
- 40 G SHAVINGS OF
  RAGUSANO DOP CHEESE
- BLACK PEPPER
- BASIL
- SEED OIL FOR FRYING
- SALT

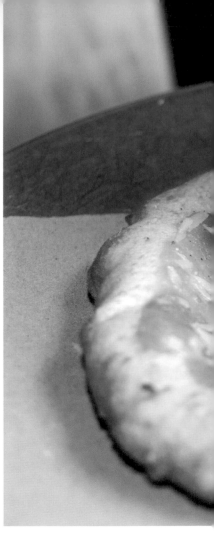

MONTANARA
ALLA GENOVESE

PREPARING YOUR INGREDIENTS

First you have to prepare your "fake" Genovese sauce, a typical dish from the Campania region. Peel and slice the copper-skinned Montoro onions, then clean and dice the celery and carrots and put the onions, celery and carrots into a large pot along with the olive oil and a basil leaf. Cover and cook for an hour, stirring every once in a while with a wooden spoon. Once the onions have released all their liquid, uncover the pot and let the water evaporate. Once all the liquid is gone, pour in enough white wine to cover the vegetables and cook for another hour. Add salt and pepper to taste and let your sauce rest for an hour with the heat turned off. In a separate pot with high sides warm up a generous amount of seed oil for frying.

PREPARING YOUR DOUGH

Using a dough scraper lift the dough off your work surface and quickly sprinkle it with flour, then place it back on your work surface. Bring your hands together over the centre of the dough, and keeping your thumbs raised, use just your fingers to gently press the dough out evenly, making sure to move from the centre out to the edges. Press out the whole circle

of dough, even the edges, and then place it on a floured plate
in preparation to fry it.

COOKING

Gently slip the dough off of the plate and into the hot oil. Using a
skimmer ladle some of the oil over the pizza until it is golden on one
side. Then flip it over and repeat until it is golden on both sides. Remove
the pizza from the oil and place it in a large colander or a dish lined with
kitchen roll to drain away the excess oil.

FINISHING TOUCH

Put the fried pizza on a plate and ladle over a generous amount of "fake"
Genovese sauce. Decorate with shavings of Ragusano DOP cheese, freshly
ground pepper, basil and a touch of extra virgin olive oil.

! SALVATORE & FRANCESCO SALVO

SAY

Choose your ingredients
carefully. Make sure they
are good quality, authentic,
healthful and in season!

SALVATORE & LUCIANO DE ANGELIS
FROM FRATELLI ZOMBINO

The two brothers Salvatore and Luciano De Angelis, both "pizzaioli", live in the famous Vomero neighbourhood of Naples. Salvatore is 42, but he started out as a kitchen boy when he was just a kid at the historic "Di Matteo" pizzeria near the courthouse, where he learned at the feet of the master "pizzaiolo" Cacialli. The brothers welcome their clients with traditional pizzas and delicious fried pizzas. This pizzeria has a classic, rustic feel to it and is always welcoming. They use the most authentic of ingredients in their effort to respect the ancient traditions that their name alludes to.

"Pizza should be made when you really want to eat it. The greatest source of inspiration for a cook is his appetite!"

Would you like to hear the story of how the two brothers got their strange nickname? Well, it all started in 1967 when Salvatore and Luciano's maternal uncles Mario and Vincenzo (both "pizzaioli") turned their humble kitchen into a real pizzeria. The patrons started calling Mario by the nickname "zombie" because of how he looked (he was very tall and pale), and soon enough both brothers became known as the Zombino brothers. The nickname started when they were young, but it has stuck with them to this day.

ingredients

- 1 BALL OF DOUGH (FOR DOUGH RECIPE SEE P. 167)
- 150 G CANNED PEELED SAN MARZANO TOMATOES
- 100 G AGEROLA FIORDILATTE CHEESE
- 50 G SLICED SPICY NEAPOLITAN SALAMI
- EXTRA VIRGIN OLIVE OIL
- GRATED PECORINO CHEESE
- BASIL
- SALT

 DIAVOLA

PREPARING YOUR INGREDIENTS

Put the San Marzano tomatoes into a bowl and mash them with your hands, then salt to taste.
Cut the fiordilatte into matchsticks and let any excess water drain out. Wash the basil and remove the leaves from the stems.

PREPARING YOUR DOUGH

Using a dough scraper lift the dough off your work surface. Quickly sprinkle it with flour and place it back on your work surface. Bring your hands together over the centre of the dough, and keeping your thumbs raised, use just your fingers to gently press the dough out moving from the centre toward the edges. Make sure not to press down the half inch closest to the edge – this is where the air bubbles will gather to form a nice cornicione. Stretch the pizza out by rotating your hands, always making sure not to press down on the edge.

PREPARING YOUR PIZZA

Using a spoon spread the tomatoes over the dough. Layer over the slices of salami and some fresh basil. Cover the pizza with fiordilatte cheese, sprinkle grated pecorino on top and drizzle with olive oil.

COOKING

Cook in a wood-fired or regular oven (see p. 170).

ingredients

- 2 SMALL BALLS OF DOUGH, EACH ABOUT HALF THE SIZE OF A NORMAL BALL (FOR RECIPE SEE P. 167)
- 1 SAUSAGE
- 80 G FRESH RICOTTA
- 60 G SMOKED FIORDILATTE CHEESE
- GRATED PECORINO CHEESE
- A BUNCH OF RAPINI (BITTER NEAPOLITAN BROCCOLI)
- GARLIC
- EXTRA VIRGIN OLIVE OIL
- BASIL
- BLACK PEPPER
- SEED OIL FOR FRYING
- SALT

FRIED CARRETTIERA WITH SAUSAGE AND RAPINI

IC

PREPARING YOUR INGREDIENTS

Wash the rapini and destem them, set aside the stems and the florets. Wash the leaves again and sauté them in a frying pan with olive oil and garlic, starting at a low flame and once they have wilted raise the temperature for a minute and cook them uncovered. Add salt and pepper to taste. Now it's time to cook the pork sausage. Start by parboiling it and then sauté it in a frying pan with a bit of olive oil and a clove of garlic. Puncture the sausage a few times and let it cook for several minutes covered, turning the sausage over a few times so that it cooks evenly. Then add the rapini leaves into the sausage pan and let them simmer together for another couple of minutes. Cut the smoked fiordilatte into matchsticks and let any excess water drain out. Mix the ricotta with a wooden spatula and add salt and pepper to taste. Wash the basil and remove the leaves from the stems. Heat the oil for frying in a pot with high sides.

PREPARING AND STUFFING YOUR DOUGH

Using a dough scraper lift the dough off your work surface and quickly sprinkle it with flour, then place it back on your work surface. Bring your hands together over the centre of the dough, and keeping your thumbs raised, use just your fingers to gently shape the dough into a large flat circle, pressing evenly all the way to the edge. Repeat with your second ball of dough. Place

a handful of rapini and sausage at the centre of each disc of dough, then layer over the fiordilatte and some grated pecorino cheese. Fold each disc in half to get a half-moon shape, and using your fists press the edges together and create a good seal.

COOKING

Take one of your pizzas and gently lower it into the oil that you have already heated to 180 °C (356 °F). Use a skimmer to pour hot oil over the surface of the pizza while holding it in place with a long spoon. Once it has turned golden on one side, turn the pizza over in the oil so it turns golden on the other side. Remove the pizza from the oil and place it on a plate lined with kitchen roll to gather any excess oil. Then, repeat with the other pizza.

FINISHING TOUCH

Decorate each pizza with a spoonful of ricotta, a sprig of basil and some ground black pepper.

} ① PORCINA

ingredients

- 1 BALL OF DOUGH (FOR DOUGH RECIPE SEE P. 167)
- 150 G SMOKED MOZZARELLA DI BUFALA
- 60 G PORCINI MUSHROOMS SAUTÉED
- FINELY CHOPPED PARSLEY
- GRATED PECORINO ROMANO CHEESE
- PINE NUTS
- RAISINS
- 4 SLICES OF DRY-CURED PROSCIUTTO (CRUDO)
- BALSAMIC VINEGAR REDUCTION
- DRY MARSALA WINE (OPTIONAL)
- BLACK PEPPER
- EXTRA VIRGIN OLIVE OIL
- SEED OIL FOR FRYING
- SALT

PREPARING YOUR INGREDIENTS

Cut the smoked mozzarella into cubes and let any excess water drain out. Toast the pine nuts in the oven. Soak the raisins, ideally in dry Marsala wine. Deep fry the slices of prosciutto; when they have become crunchy remove them from the oil and place them on a plate lined with kitchen roll.

PREPARING YOUR DOUGH

Using a dough scraper lift the dough off your work surface. Quickly sprinkle it with flour and place it back on your work surface. Bring your hands together over the centre of the dough, and keeping your thumbs raised, use just your fingers to gently press the dough out moving from the centre toward the edges. Make sure not to press down the half inch closest to the edge – this is where the air bubbles will gather to form a nice cornicione. Stretch the pizza out by rotating your hands, always making sure not to press down on the edge.

PREPARING YOUR PIZZA

Mix the smoked mozzarella cheese and the mushrooms in a bowl and season them with a pinch of finely chopped parsley and some pepper. Spread this mixture out onto the dough, keeping away from the edges. Sprinkle grated pecorino Romano cheese on top and drizzle with extra virgin olive oil.

COOKING

Cook in a wood-fired oven or regular kitchen oven (see p. 170).

FINISHING TOUCH

Take your pizza out of the oven and sprinkle the pine nuts, raisins, crunchy prosciutto and balsamic vinegar reduction on top.

} DK CONTROFAGOTTO

ingredients

- 1 BALL OF DOUGH (FOR DOUGH RECIPE SEE P. 167)
- 2 SLICES OF HAM STEAK (PROSCIUTTO COTTO)
- 80 G AGEROLA FIORDILATTE CHEESE
- 3 BREADED AND FRIED POTATO CROQUETTES
- CREAM
- GRATED PECORINO ROMANO CHEESE
- BASIL
- EXTRA VIRGIN OLIVE OIL.

PREPARING YOUR INGREDIENTS

Mash the potatoes with a masher when they are still warm. Put the potatoes into a bowl and add the egg, grated pecorino, salt and pepper. Mix the contents well, and using oiled hands shape the mixture into croquettes, approximately 5 cm (2 inches) long. Dip them in beaten egg and then in breadcrumbs, then deep-fry them in hot oil. Cut the fiordilatte cheese into matchsticks and let any excess water drain out. Wash the basil and remove the leaves from the stems.

PREPARING YOUR DOUGH

Using a dough scraper lift the dough off your work surface and quickly sprinkle it with flour, then place it back on your work surface. Bring your hands together over the centre of the dough, and keeping your thumbs raised, use just your fingers to gently shape the dough into a large flat circle, pressing evenly all the way to the edge. Now take two opposite edges of the pizza and gently pull them away from each other, creating an oval shape.

FOR THE POTATO
CROQUETTES:
- 500 G BOILED POTATOES
- ONE EGG FOR THE
  FILLING PLUS ANOTHER
  FOR THE BREADING
- GRATED PECORINO
  ROMANO CHEESE
- BREADCRUMBS
- PARSLEY
- SEED OIL FOR FRYING
- BLACK PEPPER
- SALT

PREPARING YOUR PIZZA
Using a spoon spread the cream over the centre of the
dough and layer the fiordilatte cheese and prosciutto on
top. Crumble the croquettes over the middle and sprinkle
grated pecorino Romano cheese and black pepper on
top. Bring the two narrowest sides in toward the centre
and pinch them together, leaving the pointy ends laying
flat. Drizzle olive oil over the closed part of the pizza and
sprinkle on a bit more grated pecorino Romano cheese.
Slip the pizza onto your floured pizza peel.

COOKING
Cook in a wood-fired oven or regular kitchen oven
(see p. 170).

SALVATORE & LUCIANO DE ANGELIS
SAY

Always make sure you allow excess whey to drain from the mozzarella because otherwise it could make the dough soggy during cooking.

Everyone in Naples knows each other because there is always someone, who knows someone, who knows you. if for some reason they realise they

don't know you yet, they're happy to get to know you. Relations progress quickly from a simple hello to an invitation to dinner, to an invitation to stay!

TERESA IORIO

FROM LE FIGLIE DI IORIO

As you enter this establishment, located in the heart of Naples, Teresa and her sisters will welcome you with warmth and enthusiasm. Teresa's infectious personality shines through as she says, "what you see is what you get!" She'll show you around the place and regale you with stories of her family, and what a family it is! Her father, Ernesto Iorio, had twenty children, all of them "pizzaioli", who in turn gave him 87 grandchildren and 68 great grandchildren. Teresa is the nineteenth of Ernesto Iorio's twenty children. Ernesto opened his first pizzeria, to which he gave his name, toward the end of the 1950s in Piazza Francese, part of the historical city centre of Naples. On the side, so he could pursue his passion for music, Ernesto worked as a car park attendant; he even became quite famous playing traditional Neapolitan songs in nightclubs. In his pizzeria Ernesto always wanted to make patrons feel at home, and that same spirit guides Teresa and her sisters to this day. He was a wonderful father, Teresa remembers: "When we were little our family didn't have a lot of money, but he always taught us that the good things in life, even if eaten rarely, have to be of excellent quality".

"Pizza is love. If you can feel your heart beating while you make it then it will surely be good."

Neapolitan cuisine is what really shaped the Iorio girls (le figlie di Iorio, in Italian). When they were young they used to help their grandmother knead, cook and fry. They even loved to play while sitting on the lids of pots filled with the typical dish of aubergines preserved in olive oil; their weight pressed the contents down and helped squeeze the bitterness out of the vegetables.

} **FOUR SEASONS**

ingredients

- 1 WHOLE BALL OF
  DOUGH, PLUS ANOTHER
  HALF BALL (FOR RECIPE
  SEE P. 167)
- 100 G SMOKED
  FIORDILATTE CHEESE
  CUT INTO LITTLE STRIPS
- 50 G CHERRY TOMATOES
- 40 G CANNED PEELED
  SAN MARZANO
  TOMATOES
- 30 G PROVOLONE CHEESE
- 30 G SALAMI
- 3-4 BLACK OLIVES
- 2 ANCHOVIES

PREPARING YOUR INGREDIENTS

Slice the fiordilatte and provolone cheeses and let any excess water drain out. Put the San Marzano tomatoes into a bowl and mash them with your hands, then salt to taste. Slice the little tomatoes, put them in a colander and let the water drain out. Put them into a bowl and set aside. Wash the basil and remove the leaves from the stems.

PREPARING YOUR DOUGH

Using a dough scraper lift the whole ball of dough off your work surface. Quickly sprinkle it with flour and place it back on your work surface. Bring your hands together over the centre of the dough, and keeping your thumbs raised, use just your fingers to gently press the dough out moving from the centre toward the edges. Make sure not to press down the half inch closest to the edge, where the air bubbles will gather to form the cornicione. Take the other half portion of dough and pinch off two small pieces; roll these out so that you get two long, thin strips that you can use to divide your pizza into four equal sections.

- 1 THIN SLICE OF HAM
  STEAK (PROSCIUTTO
  COTTO)
- 1 ARTICHOKE PRESERVED
  IN OIL
- BASIL
- EXTRA VIRGIN OLIVE OIL
- GRATED PECORINO AND
  PARMESAN CHEESES
- SALT

PREPARING YOUR PIZZA

Spread the San Marzano tomatoes evenly over one quarter, and sprinkle half of your fiordilatte cheese over the sauce. Put the provolone cheese and salami in another quarter. Dress your cherry tomatoes with a bit of olive oil, olives and the anchovies and lay this mixture in the third section of the dough. In the final section, lay out the remaining fiordilatte cheese and hand-torn pieces of prosciutto and artichoke.

Dust the whole pizza (except for the section with the cherry tomatoes) with a mix of grated pecorino and Parmesan cheeses. Drizzle olive oil over the whole pizza and add a few basil leaves on top.

COOKING

Cook in a wood-fired oven or regular kitchen oven (see p. 170).

} (IC) MARINARA WITH STOCKFISH

ingredients

- 1 BALL OF DOUGH (FOR
  DOUGH RECIPE SEE P. 167)
- 200 G BOILED DORSAL
  STOCKFISH MEAT (THIS
  CORRESPONDS TO THE
  HIGHEST, WHITEST PART
  OF THE STOCKFISH, AND
  SHOULD HAVE FEW
  BONES)
- 100 G CANNED PEELED
  SAN MARZANO
  TOMATOES
- 80 G CHERRY TOMATOES
- 7-8 BLACK OLIVES
- A HANDFUL OF SMALL
  CAPERS
- EXTRA VIRGIN OLIVE OIL
- GARLIC
- PARSLEY
- OREGANO
- SALT

PREPARING YOUR INGREDIENTS

Put the San Marzano tomatoes into a bowl and mash them with your hands, then salt to taste. Wash the cherry tomatoes and quarter them, then put them in a colander and let the water drain out. Put them in a bowl and set aside. Rinse the salt from the capers and remove the pits from the olives. Flake the stockfish, removing any bones. Wash and finely chop the parsley.

PREPARING YOUR DOUGH

Using a dough scraper lift the dough off your work surface. Quickly sprinkle it with flour and place it back on your work surface. Bring your hands together over the centre of the dough, and keeping your thumbs raised, use just your fingers to gently press the dough out moving from the centre toward the edges. Make sure not to press down the half inch closest to the edge – this is where the air bubbles will gather to form a nice cornicione. Stretch the pizza out by rotating your hands, always making sure not to press down on the edge.

PREPARING YOUR PIZZA

Spread the San Marzano tomatoes over the dough and then layer over the stockfish, cherry tomatoes, capers and olives. Drizzle with extra virgin olive oil and sprinkle over a pinch of oregano.

COOKING

Cook in a wood-fired oven or regular kitchen oven (see p. 170).

FINISHING TOUCH

Take your pizza out of the oven and garnish with a handful of finely chopped parsley.

PEAR

ingredients

- 1 BALL OF DOUGH (FOR DOUGH RECIPE SEE P. 167)
- 120 G SMOKED MOZZARELLA DI BUFALA
- 100 G GORGONZOLA CHEESE
- 4 SLICES OF GUANCIALE (CURED PORK CHEEK)
- 1 PEAR
- 4 SHELLED WALNUTS
- SAUTÉED ONIONS
- GRATED PARMESAN CHEESE
- THYME
- BLACK PEPPER
- EXTRA VIRGIN OLIVE OIL
- SALT

PREPARING YOUR INGREDIENTS

Slice the smoked mozzarella di bufala into wide matchsticks and let any excess water drain out. Crumble the Gorgonzola. Cut the pear into thin slices and lightly salt them. Prepare the sautéed onions: put some finely sliced onion into a frying pan with a bit of olive oil and just enough water to cover, cook until soft.

PREPARING YOUR DOUGH

Using a dough scraper lift the dough off your work surface. Quickly sprinkle it with flour and place it back on your work surface. Bring your hands together over the centre of the dough, and keeping your thumbs raised, use just your fingers to gently press the dough out moving from the centre toward the edges. Make sure not to press down the half inch closest to the edge – this is where the air bubbles will gather to form a nice cornicione. Stretch the pizza out by rotating your hands, always making sure not to press down on the edge.

PREPARING YOUR PIZZA

Lay out the slices of pear in a single layer, radiating across the entire pizza. Cover with as much of the onion mixture as you like. Sprinkle with crumbled Gorgonzola and then the smoked mozzarella. Lay the slices of guanciale over the top and finish with grated Parmesan cheese and a drizzle of olive oil.

COOKING

Cook in a wood-fired oven or regular kitchen oven (see p. 170).

FINISHING TOUCH

Take the pizza out of the oven and decorate with the shelled walnuts, thyme and freshly ground pepper.

} (DK) **THE STAR**

ingredients

- 1 BALL OF DOUGH
  (FOR RECIPE SEE P. 167)

INGREDIENTS TO FILL
THE TIPS:
- 200 G FISCELLA RICOTTA
  (COW'S MILK)
- 120 G FIORDILATTE
  CHEESE
- 1 SPOONFUL CANNED
  PEELED SAN MARZANO
  TOMATOES
- BASIL
- OREGANO
- BLACK PEPPER
- SALT

PREPARING YOUR INGREDIENTS

Cut the fiordilatte into wide strips and let any excess water drain out. Pour the ricotta into a bowl and add a pinch of salt and pepper, then mix it well with a wooden spatula. Clean and wash the rocket then cut the onion into slices. Slice the cherry tomatoes and put them into a bowl, dress them with a pinch of salt and a dash of olive oil. Wash the basil and remove the leaves from the stems.

PREPARING YOUR DOUGH

Using a dough scraper lift the dough off your work surface and quickly sprinkle it with flour, then place it back on your work surface. Bring your hands together over the centre of the dough, and keeping your thumbs raised, use just your fingers to gently press the dough out evenly, making sure to move from the centre out toward the edges. Press out the whole circle of dough but make sure not to flatten out the half inch closest to the edge because all the air bubbles produced in the dough will concentrate here to create the cornicione. Shape the dough into a circle of whatever size that you want it to be and place onto your floured pizza peel. Using clean kitchen scissors make five evenly spaced cuts into the centre of your dough that are about 8 cm deep (3 inches). Now you will have five separate sections.

PREPARING YOUR PIZZA

In each of the five sections, spread out a spoonful of ricotta, a bit of fiordilatte cheese and some basil. Now

INGREDIENTS FOR THE SALAD:

- 50 G CHERRY TOMATOES
- A HANDFUL OF ROCKET
- A SLICE OF RED TROPEA ONION
- GREEN OLIVES
- EXTRA VIRGIN OLIVE OIL
- SHAVINGS OF GRANA CHEESE
- OREGANO
- BASIL
- SALT

take the top corner of one section of dough and fold it in towards the centre of the pizza and the opposite side of that same section of dough. This way you will create a triangle; one of the tips of your star. Press the edges down with your fingers to seal them and repeat this for the remaining four sections until you have a five-pointed star. Now, paint the tips of your star with a bit of tomato sauce and drizzle over some olive oil. Sprinkle grated Parmesan cheese and oregano over the saucy tips. Spread a bit of the leftover sauce sin the circular centre of the pizza and dust it with cheese and a drizzle of olive oil.

COOKING
Cook in a wood-fired oven or regular kitchen oven (see p. 170).

FINISHING TOUCH
Take your pizza out of the oven and put your salad in the middle of the pizza, dressing it with olive oil and salt. Decorate with green olives, shavings of Grana cheese and basil.

TERESA IORIO
SAYS

Make sure to mash your
tomatoes by hand,
not in a blender.
That way they won't release all
their water and your pizza will
remain drier as it cooks.

Mission accomplished! We travelled far and wide and collected a ton of wonderful recipes, secrets and useful tips to make real Neapolitan pizza at

home. The oven is hot and the dough is cooking, we just stretched it out
and arranged all the ingredients on top. Now, all we have to do is wait.

ANTONIO & ENZO
SAY

After "stealing" so many secrets from the great "pizzaioli" of Naples, we have one last tip of our own! To make your pizza more like the ones cooked in a wood-fired oven you'll want to bake it on a refractory pizza stone and also get a wooden cutting board or pizza peel.

DOUGH TUTORIAL

ingredients

INGREDIENTS FOR SIX
BALLS OF DOUGH:

- 700-800 G TIPO "00"
  FLOUR (IF YOU CANNOT
  FIND THIS FLOUR,
  SUBSTITUTE WITH ALL-
  PURPOSE FLOUR)
- 500 G WATER
- 50 G SUNFLOWER SEED
  OIL OR LARD*
- 30 G FINE SEA SALT
- 15 G SUGAR*
- 12.5 G FRESH YEAST
  (SUBSTITUTE WITH DRY
  ACTIVE YEAST IF YOU
  CANNOT FIND FRESH
  YEAST)

MAKING YOUR DOUGH AT HOME

Pour ¾ of your flour into a large bowl; make sure it is big enough that the flour occupies no more than half of the bowl. Dissolve the salt in your water and pour this mixture into the bowl with the flour. Next, take your yeast and crumble it into the mixing bowl with the flour and water, working it together with your hands. Make sure to mix the ingredients thoroughly to avoid forming lumps. When the mixture seems homogeneous, add the remaining flour and continue to knead the dough with your hands until you achieve the right consistency, the so- called punto di pasta.

Place the dough on your work surface and knead it vigorously for approximately ten minutes, until you have reached the right consistency and can see the telltale web-like gluten structure (maglia glutinica). Shape the dough it into a single, smooth ball and place it back in into the bowl. Let it rest for 30 minutes.

DIVIDING AND SHAPING

Take a knife and cut your dough into six even pieces; each should weigh approximately 230 g. Work each piece into a ball by rolling it between your hands, which will let out any trapped air. Place the balls of dough in a clean container, spaced far enough apart so that they can grow and won't touch. Cover the container with a lid and put it in a cool, dry place for an hour. If you prefer, you can also let the dough rest on your work surface, covered with a clean tea towel.

You can also make this dough using just 1.5 g of yeast, in which case it must be left to rise for seven or eight hours. This leavening technique will give you a pizza dough that is much more fragrant, and easier to digest.

*FATS AND SUGARS
The ovens in home kitchens cannot reach the high temperatures achieved by wood-fired ovens in Neapolitan pizzerias. Consequently, a small amount of fat (seed oil, lard or extra virgin olive oil) will make your dough flakier on the outside and softer on the inside. For the same reason you want to add a bit of sugar to your dough to achieve a better crunch and colour on the crust.

9

10

11

12

13

14

15

PREPARING YOUR DOUGH

Using a dough scraper lift the dough off your work surface. Quickly sprinkle it with flour and place it back on your work surface. Bring your hands together over the centre of the dough, and keeping your thumbs raised, use just your fingers to gently press the dough out moving from the centre toward the edges. Make sure not to press down the half inch closest to the edge, as this is where the air bubbles will gather to form a nice cornicione, or frame. Stretch the pizza out by rotating your hands, always making sure not to press down on the edge.

Follow the instructions for the specific recipe you are making.

COOKING IN YOUR REGULAR KITCHEN OVEN

Place your pizza stone inside your oven and pre-heat for at least half an hour at around 250-300 °C (480-575 °F). Gently pull your garnished pizza onto your pizza peel or wooden cutting board and slip your pizza onto the pizza stone with a quick, decisive motion. Cook for four to five minutes at the same temperature. If you do not have a pizza stone you can bake your pizza on an oiled 30 cm baking pan.

TRADITIONAL COOKING IN A WOOD-FIRED OVEN

Neapolitan pizza is always cooked in a wood-fired oven.

This method of cooking gives the pizza its characteristic colours and fragrances.

A classic wood-fired oven is made from refractory stone and the floor is made of Sorrentine stone (called Biscotto). The oven, heated by the hot coals and flames, can reach temperatures exceeding 450 °C (842 °F). After shaping and garnishing their dough, pizzaioli "pull" it onto a pizza peel with a rotating motion and then plunge it into the oven, slipping the pizza onto the cooking surface with a decisive flick of their wrist. The pizza cooks for 60-90 seconds, during which time it is rotated so that all parts are exposed evenly to the heat. Stuffed pizzas are placed near the mouth of the oven to cook more slowly.

GLOSSARY

GLUTEN STRUCTURE
The gentle but decisive motion of your hands when you knead your dough makes the gluten in the flour come into contact with the water. This creates a strong, elastic and compact web that is called the maglia glutinica, or gluten structure.

LEAVENING
Dough rises, or leavens, due to the fermentation of yeast. This produces carbon dioxide, which remains trapped in the dough thanks to the gluten web created by gluten formation.

PUNTO DI PASTA
Each pizzaiolo knows just the right consistency for his or her dough, called the punto di pasta, which is a precise balance of the right ingredients, kneading and rest. You will get a feel for this when you work the dough between your hands. Look for a consistency that is elastic and soft, but not sticky.

PROOFING AND RESTING
These are processes that actually have the opposite effect of what you were trying to do when you were kneading. In this stage, the different elements of the dough (protein, starch and fat) start to break down into simpler, weaker structures that will render your dough easier to roll out, lighter, and easier to digest.

VOMERO

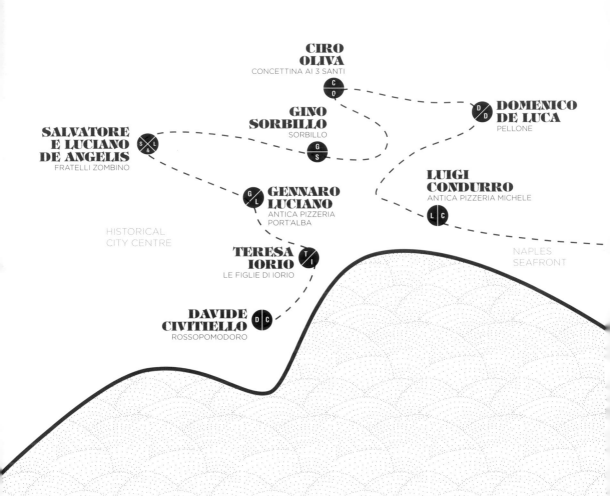

CIRO
OLIVA
CONCETTINA AI 3 SANTI

DOMENICO
DE LUCA
PELLONE

GINO
SORBILLO
SORBILLO

SALVATORE
E LUCIANO
DE ANGELIS
FRATELLI ZOMBINO

LUIGI
CONDURRO
ANTICA PIZZERIA MICHELE

GENNARO
LUCIANO
ANTICA PIZZERIA
PORT'ALBA

HISTORICAL
CITY CENTRE

TERESA
IORIO
LE FIGLIE DI IORIO

NAPLES
SEAFRONT

DAVIDE
CIVITIELLO
ROSSOPOMODORO

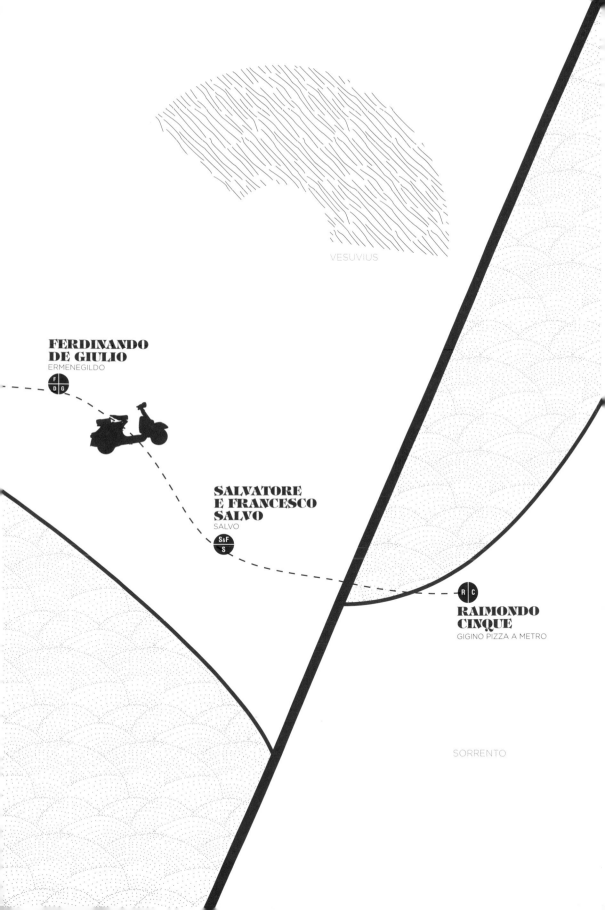

VESUVIUS

**FERDINANDO
DE GIULIO**
ERMENEGILDO

**SALVATORE
E FRANCESCO
SALVO**
SALVO

**RAIMONDO
CINQUE**
GIGINO PIZZA A METRO

SORRENTO

VOLUME CONVERSIONS: NORMALLY USED FOR LIQUIDS ONLY

Metric equivalent	Customary quantity
5 g/ml	1 teaspoon (tsp)
15 g/ml	1 tablespoon (tbsp) *or* 1/2 fluid ouncetbsp
30 ml	1 fluid ounce *or* 1/8 cup
60 ml	1/4 cup *or* 2 fluid ounces
80 ml	1/3 cup
120 ml	1/2 cup *or* 4 fluid ounces
160 ml	2/3 cup
180 ml	3/4 cup *or* 6 fluid ounces
240 ml	1 cup *or* 8 fluid ounces *or* half a pint
350 ml	1 1/2 cups *or* 12 fluid ounces
475 ml	2 cups *or* 1 pint *or* 16 fluid ounces
700 ml	3 cups *or* 1 1/2 pints
950 ml	4 cups *or* 2 pints *or* 1 quart

Note: In cases where higher precision is not justified, it may be convenient to round these conversions off as follows:

250 ml	1 cup
500 ml	1 pint
1 l	1 quart
4 l	1 gallon

Weight Conversions

Metric equivalent	Customary quantity
28 g	1 ounce
113 g	4 ounces *or* 1/4 pound
150 g	1/3 pound
230 g	8 ounces *or* 1/2 pound
300 g	2/3 pound
340 g	12 ounces *or* 3/4 pound
450 g	1 pound *or* 16 ounces
900 g	2 pounds

WEIGHTS OF COMMON INGREDIENTS IN GRAMS

Baking Powder	15 g	1 tbsp
	5 g	1 tsp
Baking Soda	15 g	1 tbsp
	5 g	1 tsp
Butter	240 g	1 cup
	30 g	1 tbsp
Corn Meal	160 g	1 cup
Corn Starch	130 g	1 cup
Egg, medium size	5 units	1 cup
	275 g	
Egg yolk, medium size	12 units	1 cup
	300 g	
Egg white, medium size	8 units	1 cup
	240 g	
Flour, all purpose	120 g	1 cup
Flour, Almond	100 g	1 cup
Flour, Bread	120 g	1 cup
Flour, Cake	110 g	1 cup
Flour, Gluten free Multi-purpose	150 g	1 cup
Flour, Rice	140 g	1 cup
Flour, Whole Wheat	115 g	1 cup
Fruits and vegetables, chopped	150 g	1 cup
Honey	340 g	1 cup
	20 g	1 tbsp
Mayonnaise	230 g	1 cup
Milk	245 g	1 cup
	250 ml	
Oil	200 g	1 cup
	222 ml	
Parmesan cheese, grated	90 g	1 cup
	11 g	2 tbsp
Potato Starch	150 g	1 cup
Salt	40 g	2 tbsp
Sugar, brown	220 g	1 cup
	14 g	1 tbsp
	5 g	1 tsp

Sugar, confectioner	120 g 8 g 3 g	1 cup 1tbsp 1 tsp
Sugar, white	200 g 12 g 4 g	1 cup 1 tbsp 1 tsp
Vegetable shortening	190 g	1 cup
Water	235 g 235 ml	1 cup
Yeast, active dry	10 g 3 g	1 tbsp 1 tsp
Yeast, fresh	10 g 3 g	1 tbsp 1 tsp
Yogurt	245 g 250 ml	1 cup

Oven temperature

°Fahrenheit	Gas Mark	°Celsius
250	1/2	120
275	1	140
300	2	150
325	3	165
350	4	180
375	5	190
400	6	200
425	7	220
450	8	230
475	9	240
500	10	260
550	Broil	290

Unless otherwise specified, all oven temperatures in this book are for conventional (static) ovens. For convection (fan-assisted) ovens, decrease the oven temperature by 25ºF (20ºC) and bake for approximately the same amount of time, but monitor closely as convection ovens can cook more efficiently. Ovens vary, so calibrate yours frequently for best results.

CONTENTS

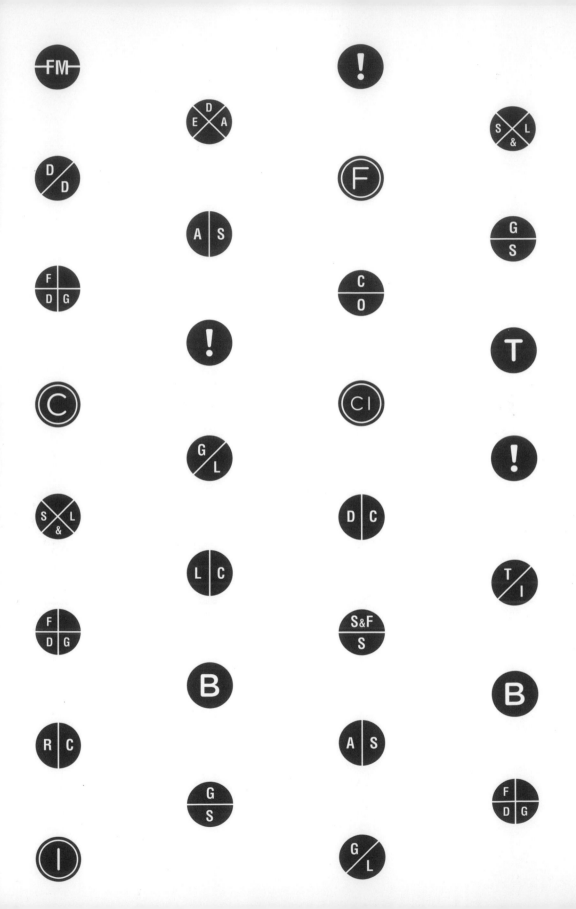